Business Rule Concepts

Getting to the Point of Knowledge

Fourth Edition

 #BRConcepts

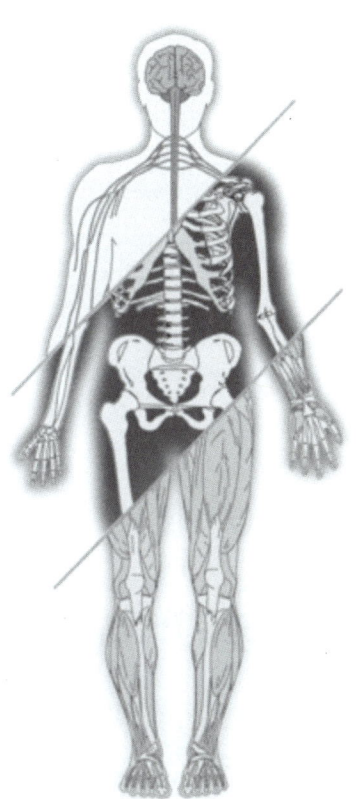

by Ronald G. Ross

Co-Founder & Principal, Business Rule Solutions, LLC
Executive Editor, BRCommunity.com
Chair, Business Rules & Decisions Forum Conference

 Business Rule Solutions, LLC

THE WORLD'S MOST TRUSTED RESOURCE FOR BUSINESS RULE
AND ENTERPRISE DECISIONING PROFESSIONALS

Academy for Business Intellect & Innovation

Business Rule Concepts
Getting to the Point of Knowledge

Fourth Edition

by Ronald G. Ross

10 9 8 7 6 5 4 3 2

ISBN 0-941049-14-0

To Vanessa

Acknowledgments

My thanks to Gladys S.W. Lam for making publication of *Business Rule Concepts* possible over so many years. Gladys is my partner and co-founder of Business Rule Solutions, LLC, and the source of many (or most) of the practical ideas in IPSpeak™ — our methodology for business rules, decision logic, and business vocabulary (concept models). Gladys is also Executive Director of the Building Business Capability (BBC) conference and Publisher of BRCommunity.com.

I would also like to thank Keri Anderson Healy, Editor of the *Business Rules Journal*, BRCommunity.com, for her editorial assistance and her many suggestions for clarifying and enhancing the content. She did that for the first-edition drafts of the material and then, unbelievably, went through the whole process yet again for the second, third, and now fourth editions.

In addition, I would like to thank Daniel Berry, University of Waterloo, for his careful reading and many helpful suggestions included in the third edition.

Also, I am indebted to all the people who have worked so hard on SBVR, a landmark standard for business vocabulary and business rules. (You know who you are.)

Finally, I would like to thank all the people who have helped make this book popular enough for now a fourth edition.

Contents

Preface

The Business Rules Paradigm

The Body Analogy

The human body is marvelous in many respects, not the least of which is its mechanics. Roughly, support for the mechanics of the human body has three basic components, separate yet intimately interconnected, as follows.

Structure is provided by the bones, which are organized and connected within the skeleton. The skeleton provides both a framework for carrying the weight of the other components as well as a semi-rigid scheme around which the other, softer components can be organized.

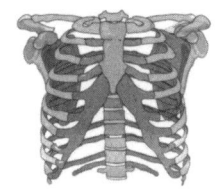

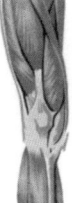

Power is provided through the muscles, which are connected to the bones. The muscles enable motion based on the framework provided by the skeleton. Since motion is what we see happening from outside the body, the muscles seem most directly responsible for the behavior we perceive.

Control is provided by the nervous system, which connects to the muscles. Nerves indirectly connect muscles to other muscles through long series of connections passing through the brain. Responses to all stimuli are coordinated through the firing of nerve impulses — no firing, no movement, and therefore no behavior.

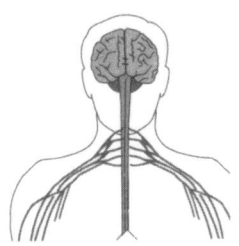

These basic mechanical components are familiar to us all. In a moment, we will see how the mechanics of business operations should be viewed in the very same way. As we examine the analogy, several observations about the mechanics of the human body are worth keeping in mind.

- All three components are *essential*. The human body literally cannot function without all three.

- The three components are all interconnected — that is, they are *integrated* with each other. For example, tendons connect muscle to bone. Successful behavior depends on this integration.

- Each of the three components is *specialized* for a particular role or responsibility. Each optimizes for its particular task. Mixing or combining the three components would provide a much less effective solution. Also, specialization provides for greater simplicity. Think about how much more complex bones would be if they incorporated muscles or how much more complex muscles would be if they incorporated nerves.

- The nervous system in some sense is the most important component because it provides coordination and control for the other two. The body is certainly capable of behavior without a well-organized nervous system — but not *effective, adaptive* behavior. Literally, you cannot operate at your best with only half a brain!

The Organization of Business Operations

We believe that business operations should be organized in a manner similar to the mechanical system of the human body. Let's revisit the three components of that system, thinking now about business operations in place of the human body.

Structure

Structure is provided by organized — that is, *structured* — knowledge about basic things in the operational part of the business. Generally, this knowledge or **know-how** consists of two kinds:

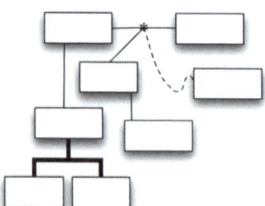

- Everyday **noun concepts** — things we refer to with nouns.

- Everyday connections we make between those noun concepts — things we often say using verbs.

These 'basic things we can know' are often simply taken for granted — just like the human skeleton in everyday activity.

Think of the noun concepts as bones, and the verb connections between them as ligaments (that is, bone-to-bone connections).

- Just as each bone has a particular shape that is optimal for its purpose and location, so too must each noun concept have a carefully-crafted 'shape'. A concept's shape is given by its **definition**, which must be clear, concise, and well-suited for its business purpose.

- Every bone or noun concept should also have a standard name. The standard name for a noun concept is a **term**.

- Each ligament also has a particular shape that is optimal for its purpose and location. Similarly, each verb connection between noun concepts must also have a standard 'shape'. These shapes are expressed by **wordings** that reference the relevant terms.

Definitions, terms, and wordings are all about meaning, the stuff of **business vocabularies**. Business vocabularies represent what we know about the operational business and how we can talk about it in an organized fashion. (From this point on in the book I will often drop the modifier "business" for "vocabulary", but I always mean *business* vocabulary.)

These days, discussion of vocabularies often falls under the heading **semantics**. Although it's fair to say this whole book is about semantics, I seldom use that term. It sounds arcane. I will generally just say *meaning* whenever the opportunity arises. There is really nothing arcane about the vocabulary of day-to-day business operations — no need for buzzwords or technical hype, just a lot of common sense.

A drawing or diagram of the complete human skeleton helps us understand how all the bones fit together. To illustrate overall vocabulary structure for a business at the operational level, it is likewise helpful to create a drawing or diagram. We call such a drawing a graphical **concept model**.

A concept model provides a framework, in many ways like a skeleton, in two basic respects.

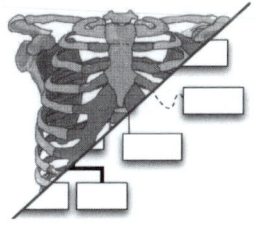

1. A concept model literally provides a structure around which the other components can be organized — that is, the 'basic things we can know' *in common* about the business at the operational level.

2. A concept model bears the 'weight' of the organization — that is, its *collective* or *shared know-how*, as put to use by its processes and business rules.

Power

Power is provided by *processes*, which operate on the structure. Whereas the concept model provides for structure, the processes provide for activity.

When we think about a business, its processes are often the first things that come to mind. Processes literally *do* what the business needs to get done (e.g., take the customer's order). However, viewing business operations as merely a collection of processes makes no more sense than viewing the human body as merely a collection of muscles. Any organism is much more than that — whether human or business.

Control

Control is provided by **business rules**, which constrain processes (the 'muscles') to act only in certain ways deemed best for the business as a whole. In the human body, there are literally hundreds of muscles, which must act in concert. If they do not, the resulting behavior won't be optimal. At worst, serious damage can result (e.g., hyperextension of a limb) that will significantly reduce the body's overall capacity to act.

Similarly, business operations encompass dozens (or hundreds) of 'muscles' (processes), which must act in concert. If they do not, the resulting behavior won't be optimal either. In some cases, serious damage can result (e.g., loss of customers, squandering of resources or opportunities, and so on) that will significantly reduce the business's overall capacity to act (that is, its competitiveness or effectiveness).

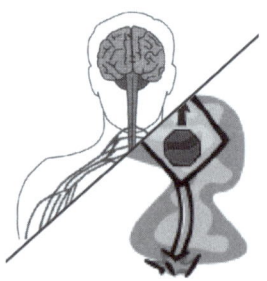

In the human body, we take many control actions of the nervous system for granted. For example, who thinks about the impulses sent to the heart to make it beat — unless, of course, something goes wrong? Or who in saying "Ouch!" thinks much about the jerk reflex that causes the hand to move so quickly off the hot stove? So long as all runs smoothly, we can apply our mental faculties to a higher purpose — whether for strategic or tactical advantage, solving a problem, or simply planning a fun lunchtime getaway.

Similarly, while operations run smoothly in the business, we can take the control provided by the business rules for granted and concentrate on matters requiring a higher degree of intelligence. Until a business rule 'breaks' somehow — and that is a very important possibility, of course — we can focus on the more creative aspects of the business.

Summary

A business is very much like a human body — a living organism.

- Structure, the skeleton, is provided by basic **noun concepts** as represented by **terms**, and verb connections between those noun concepts as represented by **wordings**.

- Power, the muscles, is provided by processes.

- Control and coordination, the nerves, are provided by **business rules**.

Let's revisit the observations I made earlier about the mechanics of the human body, now applying them to business operations.

- All three components — **concept model**, processes, and business rules — are *essential*. A business literally falls apart, disintegrates, without all three.

- The three components are obviously interrelated. For example, the processes act on knowledge about things represented in the concept model. These actions, in turn, are subject to the business rules. Successful business behavior depends on effective *integration*. These fundamental interrelationships must obviously be taken into account.

- Each of the three components is *specialized* for a particular role or responsibility and optimized for its particular task. Mixing or combining them would provide a less effective solution. Therefore the business rules need to be factored into a separate **rulebook** (automated, of course). We call this separation **Rule Independence**. As a fringe benefit comes a huge simplification in the processes. Indeed, now it is legitimate for the first time to talk of truly *thin* processes — a long-standing goal among many information technology (IT) professionals.

- In many ways business rules are the most important component since they provide control for the other two. The business and its systems are certainly capable of behavior without a well-organized set of business rules — but not *effective, adaptive* behavior. Literally, business rules are what make a business more than half-smart in how it operates.

These four observations represent the basic ideas of the *business rules paradigm*.

About this Book

This book is divided into four main parts.

Part 1: The Key Ideas

Part 1 is aimed toward the general reader seeking to understand the basic ideas of the business rules paradigm. It starts with **business vocabulary**, moves on to **business rules**, and concludes by discussing implications for the business manager or project leader. If you already have some knowledge of these things, or have read earlier editions of this book, you may find you can jump comfortably right into Parts 2–4.

Part 2: Business Vocabularies and Concept Models

Part 2 is all about business vocabularies and **concept models**. It discusses how to build a well-structured vocabulary and to represent it graphically. Concept models, a special focus of this fourth edition, support expression of business rules, IT requirements, and other forms of business communication. So the discussion picks up with *verbalization.* Concept models are also a great starting point for designing data models and class diagrams.

Part 3: Business Rules

Part 3 examines business rules in depth. The emphasis is on capture and communication of business rules in a form that is business-friendly yet robust. It explains the difference between business rules versus data or system rules. It also examines the surprising relationship between business rules and **events**. You will be guided through all the important things you need to know about business rules.

Part 4: Architecture

Part 4 explores the role business rules play in **smart architectures**, smart knowledge management, smart (*simpler*) **business processes**, and **smart** (*really* smart) **systems**. It examines **point of knowledge**, a real place — the place where business rules happen. It explains how **real-time compliance**, continuous learning, and worker empowerment are a three-in-one solution. In closing, you are invited to probe the leading edge in achieving really thin, really agile, really dynamic processes.

About ...

Business Rules Manifesto — The *Manifesto* is a two-page, 2003 work product of the Business Rules Group (BRG), laying out the basic principles of the **business rules** paradigm. For easy reference, it is published as an Appendix to this book. The *Manifesto* has now been translated into more than 15 languages. See www.BusinessRulesGroup.org.

SBVR — The formal basis for this book is given by **Semantics of Business Vocabularies and Business Rules (SBVR)**, a standard officially released in December, 2007 by the Object Management Group (OMG). The treatment of **business vocabulary** and business rules in this book is based on, and entirely consistent with, SBVR. For background on SBVR, refer to the *SBVR Insider* section on BRCommunity.com.

RuleSpeak® — All business rules in this book are expressed in **RuleSpeak** (unless noted otherwise). RuleSpeak is a business rule notation developed by Business Rule Solutions, LLC (BRS) for expressing business rules in structured natural language. It has been used directly with hundreds of business people in numerous large-scale projects beginning in the mid-1990s. RuleSpeak was one of three reference notations used in the creation of SBVR and is consistent with that standard. Basic RuleSpeak guidelines are available for free on www.RuleSpeak.com in English, Spanish, German, and Dutch, with other languages to follow.

ConceptSpeak™ — The notation used for **concept models** in this book, as well as the guidelines for defining **terms**, is based on **ConceptSpeak** (unless noted otherwise). ConceptSpeak is a set of conventions, guidelines, and techniques developed by Business Rule Solutions, LLC (BRS) for developing business vocabulary (based on SBVR). Like RuleSpeak it has been used widely beginning in the mid-1990s.

MWUD — All natural-language definitions in this book, unless noted otherwise, are from *Merriam-Webster Unabridged Dictionary* (MWUD), Version 2.5, 2000. Any emphasis appearing in these definitions has been added.

Us — We (and 'our') as used in this book refers to Business Rule Solutions, LLC (BRS). The techniques we use for business rules are embodied in **IPSpeak**™, our methodology for business rules, decision logic, and business vocabulary (concept models). The "IP" in IPSpeak stands for "intellectual property"; we believe that what this book addresses is the fundamental operational-level IP of your company.

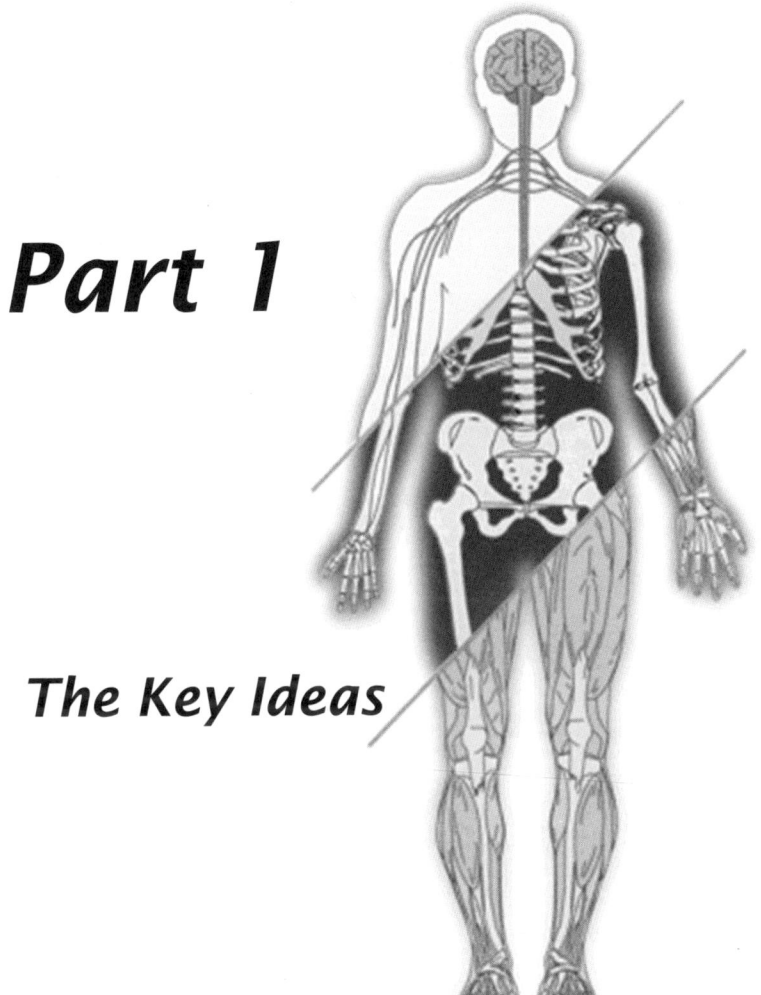

Part 1

The Key Ideas

Chapter 1

What You Need to Know About Structured Business Vocabularies

In the human body, structure is provided by the skeleton. The skeleton has two basic components: the bones and the ligaments that connect the bones. Even though the bones are larger and in a sense more basic, both components are essential.

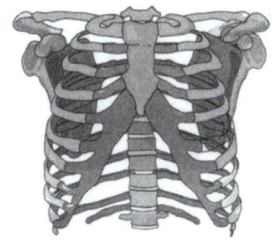

In everyday business operations, structure is given by **business vocabulary**, or more precisely by the **concepts** represented in the vocabulary. There is a whole lot more to a vocabulary than you might imagine. Without any exaggeration, a good business vocabulary is no less important to effective business operation than a strong and complete skeleton is to the human body.

Like the skeleton for the human body, a vocabulary likewise has two components: **noun concepts** as represented by **terms**, and verb connections between those noun concepts as represented by **wordings**. These noun concepts and verb connections are equivalent to bones and ligaments, respectively. They give structure to basic business knowledge — that is, they represent fundamental things in the operational business you need to know about. The terms and wordings given to them, in turn, let you talk about those things in a standard way.

We like to visualize this structure by means of a graphical **concept model**, representing the skeleton, or blueprint, for the basic knowledge needed in business operations. I will illustrate later using **ConceptSpeak**.

> Noun concepts and verb connections between them give structure to basic business knowledge. Terms and wordings let you talk about that knowledge in a standard way.

About Noun Concepts and Terms that Represent Them

A **term** is a noun or noun phrase that workers recognize and use in business communications of all kinds — for example, in agreements, deals, licenses, certifications, warranties, procedure manuals, schedules, directives, training, instructions, and so on. Business requirements for IT systems, and the documentation and help or guidance messages in operational IT systems, are additional forms of business communication.

A term carries a particular meaning for the business, which should be unambiguous given a particular context of usage. Some examples:

customer	employee name	date
prospect	delivery date due	high-risk customer
shipment	manager	employee
order	gender	line item
invoice	status	quantity back-ordered

Our meaning of *term* comes straight from *Webster's*. Note the key words *precisely limited meaning* in this definition.

Term: *a word or expression that has a precisely limited meaning in some uses or is peculiar to a science, art, profession, trade, or special subject*

Merriam-Webster's Unabridged Dictionary [MWUD]

The particular noun or noun phrase selected as a term represents merely the tip of the iceberg with respect to meaning. More fundamental is the business *concept* for which the noun or noun phrase stands. This concept *must* be defined. That is, the concept a term represents should never be taken for granted. As one practitioner put it, "The more self-evident the meaning of a term is, the more trouble you can expect." As an example, another practitioner  from a medium-sized company rattled off six different (and conflicting!) definitions of "customer" from different parts of her organization.

To communicate business rules effectively, a precise **definition** for each term should be given explicitly in business-oriented fashion, free of any IT jargon. All wordings (and statements of **business rules**) that use the term will depend on this meaning. Here is an example of a definition, again from Webster's.

Customer: *one that purchases some commodity or service; especially, one that purchases systematically or frequently*

> Every term requires a careful definition.

The core terms in the business vocabulary — those typically depicted in a graphical concept model — should satisfy these three tests:

Basic: A term should represent something fundamental to business — that is, the term should be one that cannot be derived or computed from any other terms. Any term that can be derived or computed should be specified as the subject of a business rule.

Countable: A term should represent a thing whose instances are discrete — that is, whose instances can be *counted*. A term that has an aggregate or *mass* sense (e.g., *merchandise, personnel, inventory,* and so on) should be broken down into its countable constituents (e.g., *product, employee, item,* etc.). Those are the core concepts of the vocabulary.

Non-Procedural: A term should always represent a thing we can know something about, rather than how something happens. In other words, a business vocabulary is about *knowledge*, not about the actions, processes, transforms, or procedures that produce or use that knowledge. A vocabulary, for example, might include the terms *customer* and *order*, but it would not include any action for *taking* customer orders.

The collection of all terms and definitions that satisfy the tests above are the core part of a **business vocabulary**. Such terms are crucial for expressing business rules effectively.

Basing all business rule statements on a shared vocabulary is the way to avoid a "Tower of Business Babel" when organizing business operations or developing IT requirements for systems to support them. Actually, the same is true for just about any day-to-day work product you could write. Here then is a fundamental (and obvious) principle: We will inevitably work more effectively if we all speak the same language!

> Effective business communication
> requires a shared business vocabulary.

Developing the Business Vocabulary

Core terms in a business vocabulary represent types or *classes* of things in the business, rather than **instances** of those classes. For example, a business might have 10,000 customers, but they are represented by the single term *customer*. Incidentally, since the term refers to the class rather than to all the instances, the term's singular form is preferred in the vocabulary (that is, *customer* rather than *customers*).

Business rules generally address classes rather than instances. But business rules can address instances too — for example, a business rule might apply to one country, say The Netherlands, that does not apply to another country, say Belgium.

Creating a shared business vocabulary covering both classes and pre-established instances (e.g., The Netherlands, Belgium, etc.) is an important up-front cost of doing business effectively in today's ever more knowledge-intensive world. This activity requires a measure of vision and patience.

The business benefits, however, are substantial. Managing, operating, and interacting based on agreed vocabulary is basic not only to improving business communication, but to retaining core business **know-how** as well. These are hardly luxuries in a world where staffs are ever more volatile, self-service is rapidly becoming the norm, and delivery platforms are forever evolving.

About Connections Between Noun Concepts and Wordings that Represent Them

Noun concepts can be connected to each other much as ligaments connect bones in the human skeleton. Connections between noun concepts are generally expressed using verbs and verb phrases relating appropriate terms. These noun-and-verb constructions are called **wordings** — phrases of predictable types that permit sentences, especially expressing business rules, to be made for business operations.

Examples of wordings are given in the table. Note that each wording involves a verb or verb phrase (italicized in the table) to connect relevant terms. Selection of the best verbs and verb phrases to succinctly represent connections between noun concepts is fundamental to building a robust business vocabulary.

Wording for a Connection Between Noun Concepts	Sample Business Rule Statement Using the Wording
customer *places* order	A customer has always *placed* at least one order.
shipment *is approved by* employee	A shipment must *be approved by* at least two employees.
shipment *includes* order	A shipment must not *include* more than 10 orders.

Here are some important observations:

1. Wordings extend business vocabulary in important ways. Most obvious is that wordings add standard verbs and verb phrases. Less obvious but equally important is that by connecting terms they bring structure to the vocabulary (think ligaments). For this reason, we like to say *structured* business vocabulary.

2. The sample wordings in the table actually represent types of connections, called **verb concepts**, rather than individual connections expressed as **facts**. For example, for *customer places order* a stated fact might be *Global Supply, Inc. has placed the order A601288*. Structured business vocabularies are generally more concerned with identifying verb concepts rather than expressing facts.

> **A structured business vocabulary includes wordings for verb concepts.**

3. In English and many other languages, every wording follows a strict subject-verb-object structure — for example, *customer places order*. The wording thus provides a building block for constructing sentences of arbitrary complexity that unambiguously express business rules or other kinds of knowledge.

> **A wording provides a building block for writing unambiguous sentences.**

4. A verb concept does not imply or
    establish any business rule on its own,
    nor does any associated wording. For
    example, the wording *customer places
    order* creates no business rule. It
    would be inappropriate to express a
    wording as: *A customer has always
    placed at least one order.* This latter
    statement is more than a verb concept
    — it expresses a business rule
    pertaining to the verb concept.

> A verb concept recognizes something that can be known,
> but implies no business rules on its own.

5. Verbs (e.g., *places*) used in wordings do not represent or label any
    action, task, or procedure per se (e.g., *place order*). Any such
    operation represents a different aspect of business operations — the
    power or "muscle" aspect. Think of a structured business vocabulary
    as providing the most appropriate way to organize knowledge about
    the *results* (or potential results) of such operations. By *most
    appropriate*, I mean **anomaly**-free and **semantically**-clear. In other
    words, a business vocabulary organizes what we can know (and
    communicate) as the results of operational processes or transforms
    taking place in the business.

> A structured business vocabulary organizes knowledge
> about the results of processes or transforms,
> not about how they actually take place.

6. A majority of connections of core interest for structured business
    vocabularies involve exactly two terms — e.g., *customer places order*.
    Connections involving more than two terms, however, are sometimes
    appropriate (e.g., person *visits* city *on* date). It's also possible for a
    wording to concern only a single term (e.g., person *smokes*). Refer to
    Part 2 for discussion.

7   In formal logic, each wording represents a *predicate*. More precisely,
    in **SBVR** a wording represents the *meaning* of a predicate. Although
    not directly important for practitioners, this point is a crucial one for
    engineers and others concerned with tooling and formalisms.

Certain important kinds of connections between noun concepts come in handy, *pre-defined* 'shapes'. Chapter 6 discusses four of these, two of which are illustrated briefly below. These special-purpose elements of structure extend the reach and precision of the structured business vocabulary significantly.

Special-Purpose Element of Structure	Example	Use in a Sample Business Rule Statement
Categorization	'Corporate customer' *is a **category** of* 'customer'.	A customer is always considered corporate if the customer is not an individual person.
Property	order *has* date taken order *has* date promised	An order's date promised must be at least 24 hours after the order's date taken.

A structured business vocabulary establishes the full scope of potential discourse (in business operations and any supporting systems) in a very fundamental way. If a worker or some automated process produces or expresses knowledge about some other concept or connection not in the vocabulary, we literally have no way to communicate or share such knowledge in a standard and consistent fashion.

> A structured business vocabulary establishes the basis for communicating and sharing operational business knowledge.

Using Graphical Concept Models

You might have noticed that even though structured business vocabularies are often rendered graphically, no diagrammatic examples have yet been presented. This is not because diagrams are not useful. Just the opposite is true; they are *very* useful.

Rather, I wanted to emphasize that a vocabulary is first and foremost about what we can *know*, and about how we can *communicate* about what we can know.

The bottom line is business communication. Knowledgeable workers on the business side must originate and understand the vocabulary.

> "What we can know" about the operational business can always
> be expressed on the basis of a structured business vocabulary.

Getting all the terms and wordings in a vocabulary to fit together as if in some large jigsaw puzzle can be hard. This is where a graphical **concept model** plays an important role.

When creating a blueprint for remodeling your house, you can quickly see when the pieces are not fitting together. The eye often spots the problems quite easily. A graphical concept model serves a similar purpose in developing a vocabulary. Just remember, sponsors and business people should sign off on vocabulary — the terms, definitions, and wordings — *not* on any diagram per se.

> The principal deliverable of concept modeling is
> a business vocabulary, not a diagram.

Figure 1–1 presents a simple concept model in graphical form. The various connections in this concept model are listed below it. This list includes several that are unlabeled in the diagram — these connections are based on the special-purpose elements of structure mentioned earlier.

> A concept model is a blueprint for basic business knowledge.

Figure 1–1. Sample Concept Model for a Library Using ConceptSpeak.

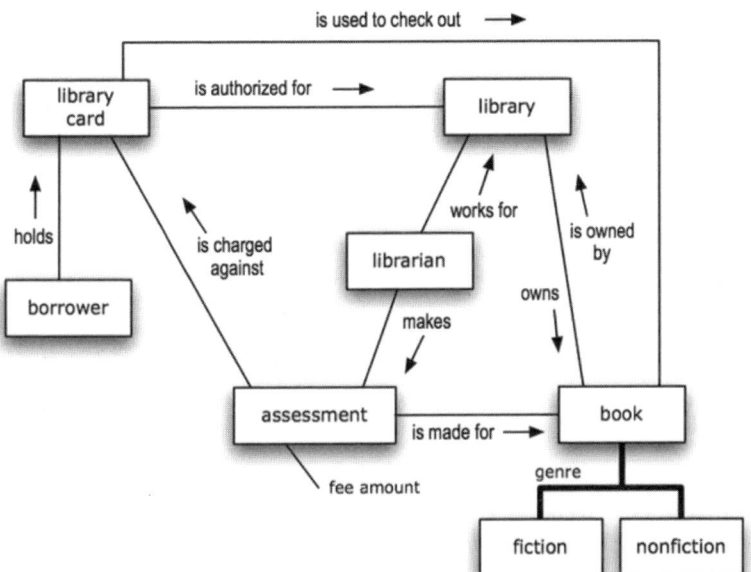

Connections in Figure 1–1

Explicitly-labeled:

- library card is used to check out book
- library card *is authorized for* library
- library *owns* book (book *is owned by* library)
- librarian *works for* library
- librarian *makes* assessment
- assessment *is made for* book
- assessment *is charged against* library card
- borrower *holds* library card

Unlabeled, based on connector type:

- fiction *is category of* book
- nonfiction *is category of* book
- assessment *has* fee amount

Closing the Communications Gap

Ask managers and workers in the business what they mean by *requirements* for developing software systems, and typically you get answers centered on functions to be performed, or on the look-and-feel of user interfaces. The answer "vocabulary" (or "shared business vocabulary") is almost never among the responses.

Nonetheless, a shared, well-structured business vocabulary is fundamental for requirements. Without such a vocabulary you cannot provide real meaning or coherency (sense) to the requirements (much less business rules).

> A shared, well-structured business vocabulary
> is fundamental for requirements.

A shared, well-structured business vocabulary literally provides *meaning* (**semantics**). This meaning, of course, is abstract. It might not be as obvious as what a system does or how the system looks on the outside. Just because something is less obvious, however, does not mean it is any less important. Break a bone, and see what happens to the body's behavior. (I have, so I can speak with some authority!)

> A shared, well-structured business vocabulary provides meaning
> and coherency to business rules and requirements.

The problem is by no means limited to communication of requirements between business workers and IT. Indeed, in many organizations today, business workers from different parts of the organization often have trouble even talking to *each other*. Or to say this more accurately, they talk to each other, but they are not really *communicating*. They live in different *semantic silos*.

A well-managed, well-structured business vocabulary should be a central fixture of business operations. We believe it should be as accessible and as interactive as, say, spellcheck in Microsoft Word.

> A well-managed, well-structured business vocabulary
> should be as accessible and as interactive
> as spellcheck in Microsoft Word.

Special care should be taken for synonyms, as well as for multiple languages. (It's a *global* world these days after all!) See the sidebar.

Note about Synonyms and Multiple Languages

In an ideal world, every operational business concept would have a single name. In real-life, of course, that's not always the case:

- The same **noun concept** can be given multiple **terms**. These terms can be in the same language producing *synonyms* (e.g., *customer, client*), in different languages (e.g., French, Mandarin, and so on), or both.

- The same **verb concept** can be given multiple **wordings**. These wordings can be in the same language (e.g., customer *places* order, order *is placed by* customer), in different languages (e.g., French, Mandarin, and so on), or both.

A robust environment for managing vocabularies must support this reality. Such support recognizes distinct contexts of usage, as well as communities with different speech preferences.

Developing and managing a shared, well-structured vocabulary means capturing business knowledge from the business-side workers and managers who possess it (or adopting it from some outside source or community of practice). The skills involved with distilling that business knowledge are essential for business analysts.

You also need appropriate business-level platforms to manage your vocabulary. Such automated support is crucial to effective business communication, as well as to organizing large sets of business rules. As discussed in Chapter 3, you will need special tooling for this purpose, which we call a **general rulebook system**.

> Your company needs an automated
> business-level work environment for managing
> its operational business vocabulary.

Summary

A good business analyst seeks to ensure that each **noun concept** and **verb concept** of the operational business is represented in the **business vocabulary**, one and only one time. The goal is to ensure that all structural components are *unified* and *unique*. This approach helps ensure that all **business rules** and other forms of business communication, including IT requirements, are expressed consistently.

> A structured business vocabulary promotes consistency.

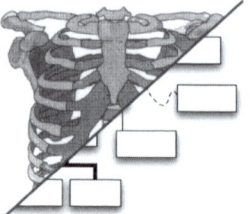

Some IT professionals believe that if they can get behavior right, the structure will simply fall into place. That is not our experience at all. It's the body as a whole that matters. You can design a lot of very elegant appendages and a lot of fancy behaviors, but there had better be a well-considered skeleton to hold them all together!

Chapter 2

What You Need to Know About Business Rules

In the human body, control is provided by the nervous system, an organized collection of nerves that connect to the muscles. Business operations must have similar coordination of behavior. This coordination or *guidance* is supported by **business rules**.

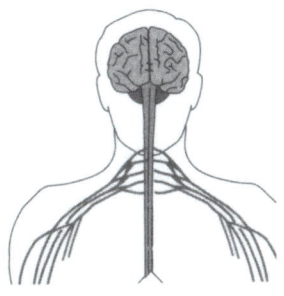

In the human body, power is provided by the muscles; in business operations, it is supported by processes. Nerves and muscles are separate; business rules and processes should be separate too.

This principle of separation is called **Rule Independence**. Not embedding business rules in processes has huge benefits — not the least of which are for the processes themselves, as discussed in Chapters 11 and 12. The ideas underlying Rule Independence are enumerated in the *Business Rules Manifesto*, a copy of which can be found at the end of this book.

> Rule Independence means separating business rules from processes.

Rules are familiar to us all in real life. We play games by rules, we live under a legal system based on rules, we set rules for our children, and so on.

Yet the idea of rules in business systems is ironically foreign to many people. Say "rules" and many IT professionals, for example, think vaguely of expert systems or artificial intelligence — approaches deemed appropriate for only very specialized or very advanced kinds of problems. Recognition has come only slowly about how central business rules actually are to basic, day-to-day business operations.

Not coincidentally, many business-side workers and managers have become so well indoctrinated in **procedural** views for developing requirements that thinking in terms of business rules might initially seem foreign and perhaps abstract. Virtually every methodology has been deficient in this regard, whether for **business process** analysis, system development, or software design.

That omission is *highly detrimental and very costly.* Thinking about the control aspect of any organized activity in terms of rules is actually very natural. For example, imagine trying to explain almost any game you can think of — chess, checkers, baseball, football, tennis, and so on — without explaining the rules on which the moves in the game are based. Even if it were possible (that's doubtful!), explaining things that way would certainly not be very *effective*.

> Absence of business rules in IT methodologies is highly detrimental and very costly for the business.

In short, you need business rules. Without any exaggeration, good business rules are no less important to business operations than a robust, finely-tuned nervous system is to the human body.

You naturally want each business rule to be specified *once and only once.* One-place specification (**single-sourcing**) means the business rule will be easier to find — and to change quickly. If you want true agility, business rules are the ticket.

Collectively, the set of business rules represents a separate **rulebook** for the business game. This rulebook should, of course, be automated, to provide scalable support for the origination and management of the business rules. As discussed in Chapter 3, you need special tooling for the rulebook, which we call a **general rulebook system**.

> The rulebook encompasses the rules of the business game.

Do business rules complicate matters for the business? *No!* Doing business is no more complicated by having independent business rules than are the games of chess, baseball, and football by having their own independent rulebooks.

Are business rules all that matter? *Of course not!* You still need artifacts for other needs, including process models, use cases, etc. These latter deliverables are needed to produce the raw power to do work — muscles for the business to flex. Business rules represent a well-developed nervous system, a way to ensure your business works *smart*.

> Business rules ensure your business works smart.

The Basics of Business Rules

A first step in understanding **business rules** is simply to relate them to the issue of guidance. The sidebar below presents a light sampling of typical business rules, each categorized informally according to the kind of guidance it provides. Note how far-ranging these categories really are. *Every* aspect of guidance for business operations can be addressed by business rules.

Restriction
A customer must not place more than three rush orders charged to its credit account.

Guideline
A customer with preferred status should have its orders filled immediately.

Computation
A customer's annual order volume is always computed as total sales closed during the company's fiscal year.

Inference
A customer is always considered preferred if the customer has placed more than five orders over $1,000.

Timing
An order must be assigned to an expeditor if shipped but not invoiced within 72 hours.

Trigger
'Send-advance-notice' must be performed for an order when the order is shipped.

A second step in understanding business rules is to understand how they relate to a **structured business vocabulary**. Rules build *directly* on **verb concepts**. Basically, expression of a business rule simply adds a sense of obligation or necessity to **terms** and **wordings** *already* set up in the **concept model**.

Terms, Facts, and Rules

The focus of **business rules** has often been described as *terms, facts, and rules.* Under the rigorous formal prescriptions of **SBVR** this mantra, which dates to the early 1990s work of the Business Rules Group (www.BusinessRulesGroup.org), is not 100% technically accurate. Nonetheless it's memorable and certainly adequate for an initial understanding.

Here is a sample business rule: *A customer must be assigned to an agent if the customer has placed an order.* Figure 2–1 shows the relevant terms and wordings for this statement. Note how the verb concepts worded *customer places order* and *customer is assigned to agent* are used directly in the statement, with only minor adjustments in tense as appropriate for English grammar.

Figure 2–1. Terms and Wordings for the Agent-Assignment Business Rule.

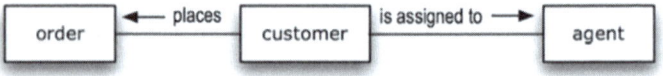

In business problems involving hundreds or thousands of business rules — not at all uncommon — there is no way to achieve consistency across such large numbers of statements without a common base of terms and wordings. This vocabulary scaffolding is indispensable for *scaling up*.

> Scaling up requires that business rules be expressed directly on a structured business vocabulary.

Basing verbalizations directly on wordings for verb concepts is a key feature of business-oriented notations for business rules such as **RuleSpeak**.

A third step in understanding business rules is appreciating the importance and power of expressing business rules **declaratively**. When statements are based directly on wordings for verb concepts, the result is always declarative. The Agent-Assignment Business Rule presented above illustrates. Expressing business rules declaratively is a key means of liberating the business from the perils of IT-speak. The sidebar below explains how you can determine whether specifications are declarative.

When Are Specifications Declarative?

In graduate school in the early 1970s, I learned this highly pragmatic test for determining whether specifications are **declarative**:

- Take each statement of the specification and type it on an individual punch card. (It's really hard to find punch cards these days, but for the sake of discussion, let's ignore that.)
- Assemble the deck.
- Test it to make sure it works.
- Throw the whole deck up in the air.
- Pick up all the cards in random order.
- Re-test it.

If the logic still works, the statements are declarative. If not, they are **procedural**. The point is that in declarative specifications no logic is lost 'between the lines' — i.e., none is intrinsic to the sequence of presentation. In other words, there is no hidden **semantics** (meaning).

Fully appreciating these ideas requires careful examination of the relationship between business rules and **events**. In general, business rules specified declaratively are free of any direct reference to events. More about that important topic in Chapter 8.

Violation of Business Rules

Let's examine more closely what should happen when a business rule is **breached**. Consider the Agent-Assignment Business Rule. What happens when an event occurs that might violate this business rule?

1. The business rule needs to be evaluated with respect to the event. We call that a **flash point**.

2. If a **violation** is detected, appropriate intervention should ensue.

3. Assuming the user is authorized and knowledgeable, some explanation should be provided about what triggered the intervention. You might call that explanation an **error message**, but we prefer **guidance message**. The intent should be to inform and to shape appropriate business behavior, rather than simply reprimand or inhibit it.

What should that guidance message say? *The default guidance message can contain exactly the same text as given for the business rule.* For the Agent-Assignment Business Rule it could literally read: *A customer must be assigned to an agent if the customer has placed an order.* To put this more strongly, a business rule statement *is* a guidance message.

A business rule statement *is* a guidance message.

Now I overstated the case a bit to make the point. Obviously, additional or customized text can be provided to explain the relevance of the business rule to the specific event, to suggest corrective measures, to give examples, and so on. Also, in a truly-friendly business rule system, you often wouldn't want simply to present the message, then shut down the work. Instead, as discussed in Part 4, you might offer a **procedure** or **script** to the user to assist in taking immediate corrective action. But for now, let's stick to the main point.

And that main point is this: The guidance messages that business workers see once an operational business system is deployed can be the very same business rules that knowledgeable workers on the business side expressed during the capture of business requirements. Guidance messages, business rule statements, error messages from a business perspective — these are all *literally* one and the same. Well-expressed business rules during the requirements process provide the basis for well-expressed guidance messages; poorly-expressed business rules during the requirements process generally result in poorly-expressed guidance messages.

This approach has *proven* potential for closing the requirements gap between business people and IT that still plagues many companies today. In traditional approaches, much is usually lost in the translation of up-front requirements into the actual running systems. Using business rules, the business side participates directly in developing what it ultimately gets back as guidance messages — a truly business-oriented approach.

Direct assistance in expressing the business rules up-front will prove very valuable to the managers and workers involved in business rule capture. It will enable them to be far more articulate about their requirements. We see the ability to assist in expressing business rules as a key skill for business analysts. Every business analyst should speak **RuleSpeak**!

> Business rules help close the requirements gap.

Decision Management and Decision Tables

Business rules directly support business operations in at least three ways:

- Guide day-to-day business activity.
- Shape operational business judgments.
- Make operational business decisions.

The former two roles coordinate **business processes**; the third role leads to decision management and **decision tables** (refer to Chapter 9).

An **operational business decision** is where some minute-to-minute, day-to-day determination must be made in performing business activity. Examples of operational decisions include whether or not to:

- Approve an application for automobile insurance.
- Pay a claim.
- Buy a stock.
- Declare an emergency.
- Accept a reservation.
- Indicate possible fraud.
- Give an on-the-spot discount to a customer.
- Assign a particular resource to a given request.
- Select a health care service for a patient.
- Certify a ship for safety.

As these examples illustrate, operational business decisions might have to do with configuration, allocation, assignment, classification, assessment, compliance, diagnosis, and so on.

Business Activity vs. Specialized Know-How

You can expect business rules to generally align according to the kind of operational support they provide — to coordinate business activity or to apply specialized **know-how**.

Examples for three different organizations are given below.

Internal Revenue Service (IRS)

Business Rule to Coordinate Business Activity

- *A processed tax return must indicate the IRS Center that reviewed it.*

Business Rule to Apply Specialized Know-How

- *The calculated total income must be computed as tax return wages (line 1) plus tax return taxable-interest (line 2) plus tax return unemployment compensation (line 3).*

Ministry of Health

Business Rule to Coordinate Business Activity

- *A claim must be assigned to an examiner if fraud is suspected.*
- *An on-site audit must be conducted for a service provider at least once every five years.*

Business Rule to Apply Specialized Know-How

- *A claim involving comprehensive visits or consultations by the same physician for the same patient must not be paid more than once within 180 days.*
- *A claim that requests payment for a service event that is a provision of health service type 'consultation' may be paid only if the service event results from a referral received from another service provider.*

Ship Inspection Agency

Business Rule to Coordinate Business Activity

- *A ship inspection work order must include at least one attendance date.*
- *A ship must indicate a client who is financially responsible for inspections.*
- *An inspection due for a ship must be considered suspended if the ship is laid-up.*

Business Rule to Apply Specialized Know-How

- *A ship area subject to corrosion must be inspected annually.*
- *A salt water ballast tank must be inspected empty if the ship is more than five years old.*
- *A barge must have an approved bilge system to pump from and drain all below-deck machinery spaces.*

Business rules concerning the company's product/service invariably involve the company's special area(s) of expertise. They often use more arcane (knowledge-rich) vocabulary. For that reason, such business rules are typically more difficult to capture and express. And there tends to be significantly more of them. Your approach needs to be prepared for that.

Summary

Business rules should be externalized from processes and established as a separate resource. **Rule Independence** permits direct management of the business rules, so they can evolve at their own natural pace rather than that of the software release cycle.

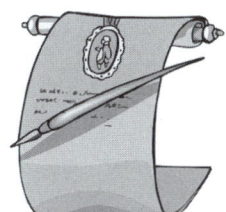

Other benefits include better process models, and much closer tie-in to the business side (a.k.a. business alignment). Business rules put your company on the road to *true* agility.

> Business rules put your company on the road to *true* agility.

When introduced to business rules, the first reaction some people have is that their business has far more **exceptions** to business rules than rules per se. They question how all these exceptions can be handled in any organized fashion. This is a valid concern.

Exceptions to business rules, however, merely represent more business rules. Looking at it that way is crucial — *every business rule costs you something.*

> Every business rule costs something.

The most significant cost of rules is not the direct cost of their implementation and maintenance in software systems (especially if you're using a rule engine). The real cost often lies hidden in the associated documentation, training, administration, and time — the *people* time it takes to communicate the business rules and to change them. Time, of course, is among the most precious of all commodities. Your business does not need *more* rules — it probably needs fewer (*good*) rules!

Chapter 3

What You Need to Know About Rulebook Management

How many **business rules** does your company have? A hundred? A thousand? Ten thousand? More? How easy is it to change any one of those rules? How easy is it to determine where the rule is implemented? How easy is it to find out why it was implemented in the first place?

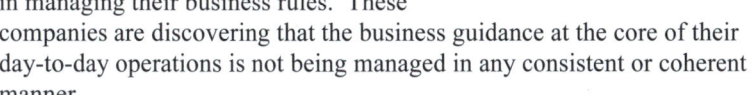

Many companies today are starting to realize they have significant problems in managing their business rules. These companies are discovering that the business guidance at the core of their day-to-day operations is not being managed in any consistent or coherent manner.

One way or another, every organization will eventually discover the need for managing its business rules. New skills must be acquired and appropriate work environments implemented. Fortunately, pioneering companies have already discovered what these techniques are, and good commercial tools have emerged to support them. These tools and techniques are already paying off handsomely.

General Rulebook Systems (GRBS)

We call the kind of automated, specialized, business-level platform your company needs to manage its business rules a **general rulebook system (GRBS)**. The purpose of a GRBS is to record, develop, and coordinate business rules, but not 'execute' them per se. Think of a GRBS as more or less the counterpart of a general ledger system, except that the GRBS is for business rules.

> A *general rulebook system* (GRBS) is an automated, specialized, business-level platform for managing business rules.

What should a general rulebook system (GRBS) look like? In one sense, a GRBS is simply a database or repository — one whose interfaces must be business-friendly. What should be recorded in it? What additional kinds of support are needed?

Remember that business rules represent business-level guidance — not programming logic or rules specified for implementation under a rule engine or other software platform. The goal is to give *business* workers and *business* analysts the ability to access and manage the guidance directly. So the focus should be on the kinds of challenges these business workers and analysts face on a day-in, day-out basis.

Repositories supporting IT professionals doing requirements development or rule authoring under rule engines do not measure up in that regard. Most were engineered primarily for use by IT staff with the goal of designing software applications. The difference is not a trivial one.

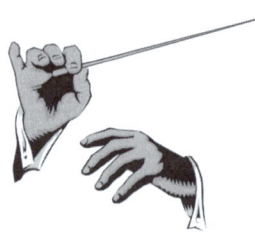

Fundamental to supporting *business*-level business rules is an integrated capability to manage **business vocabulary** and **concept models**. When rules number in the thousands — or even 'just' in the hundreds — coordinating vocabulary is essential. Imagine trying to understand and apply that many business rules without such coordination. It's hard to emphasize too much the need for business-level coordination of business vocabulary.

Traceability and Corporate Memory

Many questions about business rules (and business vocabulary) that business workers and business analysts will have are quite predictable. Frequently asked questions about business rules, including business rules organized as **decision tables**, are listed in Table 3–1. Although the importance of these questions is self-evident, most companies have never managed this kind of core knowledge in any coordinated or comprehensive manner.

Table 3–1. FAQs a General Rulebook System (GRBS) Should Support.

- *To which areas of the business does a business rule apply?*
- *What work or decision-making tasks does a business rule guide?*
- *Where is a business rule implemented?*
- *In what jurisdictions is a business rule enforced?*
- *What purpose does a business rule serve?*
- *When was a business rule created?*
- *When did a business rule become effective?*
- *Where and when has the business rule been published?*
- *Are there previous versions of a business rule?*
- *Is a business rule currently in effect?*
- *Has a business rule been retired or replaced, and if so, when and why?*
- *Who is responsible for a business rule?*
- *What influenced the creation or modification of a business rule?*
- *Who can answer particular kinds of questions about a business rule?*
- *Who has been involved with a business rule over time, and in what way?*
- *Has the business rule been adopted by, or from, some outside community of practice?*
- *Where can more information about a business rule be found?*

Another question crucial to **rulebook management** is being able to address relationships *between* business rules — that is, to easily trace rule-to-rule connections. Business rules can be interconnected in many ways, but the most important are:

- A rule has been interpreted from or into another rule.
- A rule acts as an **exception** to another rule.
- A rule supports a computation or derivation used by another rule.

The first kind of connection above is particularly important. Many business rules are interpretations of what we call **governing rules** — laws, acts, statutes, regulations, contracts, agreements, deals, **business policies**, certifications, licenses, and so on. Knowing the *who*, *when*, and *why* of such interpretations is crucial in supporting impact assessment when a rule changes. By the way, most business rules do change, sooner or later!

In today's world, discovering or reconstructing the pedigree of a business rule is time-consuming, error-prone, and sometimes impossible. Worse, once discovered or reproduced for a particular need at a point in time, the history is often not retained in any organized fashion for future use. That means the whole process must be repeated the next time it is needed, *ad nauseam*.

To be blunt, our **corporate memory** about business rules is deeply flawed. And consider this — without memory there can be no *accountability*.

What we have today is actually a risky and very expensive way to do business. The valuable resources consumed could certainly be put to better use. Think of rulebook management as a practical means to create pinpoint corporate memory, always keeping it right at your fingertips.

> Rulebook management is about creating pinpoint corporate memory, always keeping it right at your fingertips.

All the items listed in Table 3–1 illustrate various forms of *traceability*. A GRBS can provide basic support for traceability by means of predefined reports and queries. Beyond that, visualization techniques are quite useful for presenting more complex or highly-interrelated information. Comprehensive support for business-side traceability is a key ingredient in successful rulebook management.

Rulebook Management: the skills, techniques, and processes needed to express, analyze, trace, retain, and manage **business rules** used for day-to-day business operations

Focus: Manage business rules as a business problem rather than a technical problem.

Goals: Ensure that ...
- Basic business **know-how** is always accessible to those duly authorized.
- **Business policies**, regulations, contractual obligations, etc. are interpreted in a faithful, repeatable, and transparent fashion.

Another important aspect of rulebook management is the difficulty of validating large sets of business rules, and ensuring that the logic they represent is complete, internally consistent, and non-redundant. Automated support in this area is a *must have*. Examples of *quality* items:

- A rule is similar to another rule.

- A rule subsumes another rule.

- A rule is logically equivalent to another rule.

- A rule is in **conflict** with another rule.

Rather than a new chore for the company's thinly stretched resources, such support should be viewed as an important new area of efficiency. Never before has the company's business rules been in a form that could be checked *before deployment* for true quality by business workers and business analysts from the business point of view.

> Your general rulebook system (GRBS)
> must provide automated quality assessment
> for use by business workers and business analysts.

Smart Governance

Say "governance" and many people immediately think IT governance, or sometimes data, process, or architecture governance. **Governance** has been bandied about so much that its meaning has become clouded and trivialized. That's unfortunate, because the true meaning of governance is actually straightforward. And that true meaning has everything to do with meeting today's business challenges.

So bear with me while I do a little refresher on the meaning of "governance". You may be surprised at what pops out! Here's how *governance* is defined in MWUD:

> **Governance** ...
> 1: the act or ***process*** of governing
> 2a: the office, power, or ***function*** of governing
> 2b: controlling or directing influence : AUTHORITY
> 3: the state of being governed
> 4a: ***the manner or method*** of governing : conduct of office
> 4b [obsolete]
> 5: ***a system*** of governing

So "governance" implies the *process, function, manner or method,* or *system* of governing. It also implies *authority* or the *state of being governed.* Since most of the definitions reference "governing", let's also examine *govern* in MWUD. Note how prominently 'rule' and 'policy' appear in these definitions.

> **Govern** ...
> *transitive verb*
> 1a: to exercise arbitrarily or by established **rules** continuous sovereign authority over; especially: to control and direct the making and administration of **policy** in
> 3a: to control, direct, or strongly influence the actions and conduct of (as a person or a group)
> *intransitive verb*
> 1: to prevail or have decisive influence : CONTROL
> 2: to exercise authority: perform the functions of government especially in the making and execution of **policy**

At the risk of saying the obvious, note that the definitions do not say anything about IT, data, or anything similar. For that matter, they don't even mention processes(!). The definitions do, however, have everything to do with business rules. To demonstrate, take a quick look at the seminal definition of "business rule" from the original GUIDE report in 1995. Note the key words 'control' and 'influence'.

> **Business Rule** [GUIDE, 1995] ... a statement that defines or constrains some aspect of the business ... [which is] intended to assert business structure, or to **control** or **influence** the behavior of the business

The newer definition of 'business rule' in **SBVR** is based on the following definition of *rule* from the Oxford Dictionary of English. Note the pivotal place of *governing*.

> **Rule**: one of a set of explicit or understood regulations or principles **governing** conduct or procedure within a particular area of activity … a law or principle that operates within a particular sphere of knowledge, describing, or prescribing what is possible or allowable

Here is my point. Business rules and governance are inherently and inextricably linked. The better your company gets at business rules, the better (smarter) it can become at the nuts and bolts of governance. Simple as that. And absolutely as critical as that in a volatile, rapidly changing, and ever more complex (and regulated) world!

What Business Governance Is and How Rulebook Management Relates to It

So what do we mean by **business governance**? A key phrase in the definition of *govern* is: "… the making and administration of policy in." Central to the activity of governing then are:

- How policy and rules are created ("made").
- How policy and rules are deployed (managed, distributed, and monitored) within the actual day-to-day operations of the business ("administration").

Accordingly, our definition for *business governance* is:

> **Business Governance** … a process, organizational function, set of techniques, and systematic approach for creating and deploying policy and business rules into day-to-day business operations

The effectiveness of business governance clearly hinges on the ability to deploy policy and business rules effectively. Such deployment should be *timely, effective, selective, pervasive, traceable, repeatable,* and *retractable.* We also want the activity to be transparent and to be able to hold accountable those parties responsible for specific actions.

For effective deployment, all four aspects mentioned above — a *process, organizational function, set of techniques,* and *systematic approach* — are essential. Given the complexity of the activity, however, the one perhaps most basic is simply having a *systematic approach.*

That's where **rulebook management** comes to play. As discussed earlier, your company needs a **general rulebook system (GRBS)**. In the context of business governance, a GRBS plays another critical role: *knowledge retention.*

You *will* lose workers. Staff will be downsized or outsourced; your baby boomers will retire; your most critical subject matter expert will win the lottery. If your business rules have not been retained and managed, how do you regain the lost knowledge? One approach is to try to mine business rules from legacy code or spreadsheets (not a fun prospect!). Far better — just don't lose the business rules in the first place!

> Never lose your business rules!

So job one in moving toward smarter governance is acquiring and implementing a general rulebook system (GRBS). That gives you your systematic approach. Then you can start talking seriously about revitalizing the process of business governance.

Revitalizing the Governance Process

Yes, Virginia, there is a **governance process**. Unfortunately, in many companies today the as-is governance process is ad hoc, ragged, and effectively broken. That just won't do, given the complexity, rate of change, and knowledge-intensity of doing business in today's high-tech, globally-connected world. Thinking in the large, how to fix the nuts-and-bolts of the governance process in a highly pragmatic fashion is the most fundamental insight and value-add of the business rules paradigm.

> In many companies today,
> the governance process is effectively broken.

The governance process involves a series of actions and checkpoints indicating who should be doing what, and when, with respect to deploying policy and business rules. The scope of the governance process includes, but is not limited to:

- Developing internal **business policies**.
- Evaluating relevant laws, regulations, contracts, agreements, etc.
- Tracing interpretations for both the above.
- Performing reviews.
- Resolving **conflicts**.
- Coordinating sign-offs.
- Performing impact assessments.
- Coordinating business roll-out (deployment) of new or modified **business rules**.
- Ensuring the correctness of system-level deployments from the business perspective.
- Assessing when to retract or retire business rules.

A revitalized governance process should view the work from beginning-to-end, encompassing all seven of these tasks:

The Seven Steps of the Governance Process
1. *Assess/review business influences.*
2. *Create/refine business strategy.*
3. *Develop operational business rules.*
4. *Assess/simulate impact.*
5. *Deploy business rules.*
6. *Monitor performance.*
7. *Revise/retire business rules.*

Note the starting points in tasks 1 and 2. These have to do with injecting structured strategy into the governance process. Can strategy really be structured and effectively documented? Absolutely. Refer to [Lam 1998], [The Business Motivation Model], and [Ross and Lam, 2011, Chapter 4].

Who should have responsibility for the governance process? Processes need engineering (or more commonly, re-engineering) and for that you need engineers. The governance process specifically needs engineers specializing in governance — *governance engineers*. What goals should they have? All the items in Table 3–2. Ultimately, *this* is what rulebook management is all about.

Table 3–2. Goals for Governance Engineers.

- **Fiduciary Responsibilities Support.** Demonstrate compliance by officers of the organization with their fiduciary responsibilities.
- **Risk Management.** Enable more effective, timely, and focused management of risks by monitoring performance around critical items of business policy and strategy.
- **Liability Management.** Reduce or eliminate legal and financial liabilities due to non-compliance with contractual obligations and statutory responsibilities.
- **Quality Assurance.** Ensure consistency in business behavior, and appropriate interactions with external stakeholders.
- **Regulatory Compliance.** Ensure conformance with external regulation.
- **Agility.** Ensure timely and coordinated deployment of changes in business policy and strategy.
- **Knowledge Retention.** Ensure that specialized know-how, operational business intellectual property (IP), and core competencies are captured and managed explicitly, so that survivability and sustainability are less dependent on individual workers and their tacit knowledge.
- **Accountability.** Ensure clear lines of responsibility for interpretations and deployments of governing rules into day-to-day operations.
- **Transparency.** Ensure that business activity subject to external regulation is conducted in a manner that can be fully audited.

Summary

Business rules and **business vocabulary** should be managed in concert. Associated tasks are very unlike managing requirements and the artifacts of software development and should not be mixed together. The former should be undertaken purely as a business proposition, using a **general rulebook system (GRBS)**.

Business rules and the **governance** of the enterprise are inherently and inextricably linked. The implication is that the better your company gets at business rules — and **rulebook management** — the better it can become at the nuts and bolts of governance. The goal — *smart* governance.

| The goal — *smart* governance. |

Part 2

Business Vocabularies and Concept Models

Chapter 4

Concept Models and Verbalization

Let me tell you something we have learned from our work on business rules. The world's leading cause of ambiguity in expressing business rules — and requirements — is *missing verbs*. The following example illustrates.

> Business Rule: *An order must not be shipped if the outstanding balance exceeds credit authorization.*

As a first-cut statement, that's perhaps not bad. The more you read it, however, the more ambiguity you'll see. Clearly, some important ideas are hidden or missing. For example:

- The outstanding balance *of what?* ...order? ...customer? ...account? ...shipment?
- The credit authorization *of what?* ...order? ...customer? ...account? ...shipment?

The hidden or missing ideas are all verb-related. To eliminate the ambiguity, the relevant **verb concepts** must be discerned, then the original **business rule** restated. Suppose the relevant verb concepts can be worded as follows:

customer places order

customer has credit authorization

customer holds account

account has outstanding balance

Using **RuleSpeak** the business rule can now be restated as:

> Revised Business Rule: *An order must not be shipped if the outstanding balance of the account held by the customer that placed the order exceeds the credit authorization of the customer.*

Although the resulting statement is a bit wordier, it is far less likely to be misunderstood, misapplied, or mis-implemented. It is now *enterprise-robust*. Key insights:

1. **Wordings** for verb concepts are naturally expressed using verbs. Note in particular the verb *holds* (or *held*) and the verb *places* (or *placed*). I'll come back to the pesky preposition 'of' later.

2. Wordings for relevant verb concepts should always appear *explicitly* in expression of business rules. For that matter, wordings should appear explicitly in *any* form of business communication you want to be unambiguous, including IT requirements.

> To reduce ambiguity in written business communication of all types, including business rules, you must use standard verbs.

Given that verbs are so crucial to effective business communication of all kinds, you might question why data models and class diagrams haven't focused more directly on them. The answer, quite simply, is that these tools weren't created for that purpose. They are first and foremost *design* tools for IT professionals.

What do IT professionals design? In general, they are focused on implementing data containers (e.g., tables) or software objects. That focus leaves them noun-ish, but not also verb-ish. The price we are paying for that shortfall in poor business communication practices is huge.

How can the problem be fixed? The answer is simply that verb-ish things should be included alongside noun-ish things as a fundamental part of any structural modeling.

What It Means to be Verb-ish

Many IT professionals associate verbs only with processes, as in "take order" or "pay invoice" or "hire employee". Nothing in the real-world meaning of 'verb', however, limits its use solely to that concern. Have a look at the MWUD definitions of 'verb' and 'predicate' in the box below. Restricting use of verbs only to the naming of processes, tasks, or actions is very unnatural.

> **Verb:** *a word belonging to that part of speech that characteristically is the grammatical center of a <u>predicate</u> and expresses an act, occurrence, or mode of being ...*
>
> **Predicate:** *[2] the part of a <u>sentence</u> or clause that expresses what is said of the subject and that usually consists of a verb with or without objects, complements, or adverbial modifiers*

Experts in the field of linguistics explain that verbs play a far more crucial role. For example, Steven Pinker says, "A verb, then, is not just a word that refers to an action or state but the chassis of a <u>sentence</u>. It is a framework with receptacles for the other parts ... to be bolted onto" [Pinker 2007, p. 31, emphasis added]. Without verbs, literally there are no sentences.

Sentences are how you communicate effectively. Sentences are what you're reading *right now*. A well-written business rule is always a sentence. In general, all business communication and many forms of business requirements should be sentences. When you start looking at things that way, it becomes obvious that verbs must be an integral part of *any* structural model.

> A well-written business rule is always
> a sentence based on standard verbs.

Let's take a closer look. Without going too deep into philosophical questions, every verb generally has two sides. Yes, you can think of a verb as designating some action. But you can also think of a verb as designating something you can *know*. Take, for example, the verb 'to place', as in a customer *placing* an order. You can look at 'to place' from two perspectives, both valid:

- There is something a customer can <u>do</u> — i.e., *place* an order. That's an <u>action</u> or <u>process</u>.

- There is something that can be <u>known</u> — i.e., that a customer *can place* an order. That's a **fact**; something you can <u>know</u>.

The first perspective, of course, is very important. No one is saying you shouldn't model processes. But even a cursory look at other challenges facing businesses today suggests the second perspective is also crucial.

Verbs are therefore the point of departure for addressing a host of broader needs facing businesses today. Modeling the underlying verb concepts (as well as the nouns they involve) is the purpose of **concept models** or *fact models*. Think of a concept model as a *verbal* model, one serving for more effective *verbalization* of operational business knowledge. It's high time we focus on the basics of business communication as the starting point for everything we do or design.

> A concept model is a *verbal* model, one serving for more effective *verbalization* of operational business knowledge.

Fortunately, concept modeling as a discipline has a long and solid pedigree. It's not something new; it's been around for decades. The gurus of this space include Terry Halpin [Halpin 2008] and Sjir Nijssen [Nijssen 1981]; the standard for the space is **SBVR**. Actually, the discussion in this book features only two new things:

1. **RuleSpeak** and the now in-depth understanding of how business rules should be based on verb concepts and concept models.

2. The conventions used to represent concept models graphically. We developed this graphical notation in large-scale client projects starting in the mid-1990s to provide a more business-friendly face for concept models.

Issues That Can Only Be Handled Well Using Verbs

Traditional data models and class diagrams fall short in a number of respects in their handling of verbs. The following discussion outlines three of these shortcomings, each addressed effectively in concept modeling. First, two quick points about terminology in the box below.

> **Verb:** For convenience, I say *verb* although I really mean *verb or verb phrase*. For example, 'owns' counts as a verb, but so too do 'rides in' and 'is being actively marketed'.
>
> **Verb Concept:** A **verb concept** is always understood to include some relevant **noun concept(s)** as well as a verb. So the verb 'owns' might be included in the expression of the verb concept 'person *owns* vehicle'.

Unary Verb Concepts — Verbs about Only One Thing

A **unary verb concept** always provides a simple yes-or-no answer to some basic operational business question. In other words, a unary verb concept is always Boolean (i.e., true or false). The following example illustrates.

Figure 4–1. Concept model showing unary verb concept.

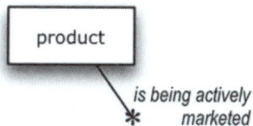

> **Note on ConceptSpeak Notation**
> The starburst symbol always indicates 'verb concept'. Here, the starburst introduces the verb (phrase) 'is being actively marketed'. The line between the noun concept 'product' and the starburst means nothing on its own; it simply shows where the verb (phrase) fits into the diagram.

The verb concept worded 'product is being actively marketed' is unary because it pertains to only one noun concept, product. This unary verb concept indicates that a given product either is or is not being actively marketed. The *actual* answer to the question, of course, depends on which particular product is being talked about.

Like any verb concept, this unary verb concept could be relevant to many kinds of business communications, including statements of business rules. The following sample business rule illustrates.

> Business Rule: *A briefing may be given only for a product that is being actively marketed.*

Roles — Noun Concepts Whose Meaning Is All Tied Up with Verbs

Business people often have a special **term** for a noun concept they use only in the context of some particular verb concept. The following example illustrates.

Figure 4–2. Concept model showing a role.

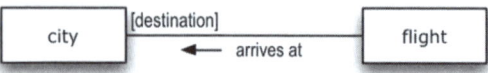

The verb concept diagrammed above is: *flight arrives at [destination] city*. The term in brackets, 'destination', is simply a more specific term used to refer to a city when it is a city where a flight arrives. Such a **role** name designates the part (or 'role') the concept 'city' plays in the context of the verb concept. It means nothing more than that.

Note on ConceptSpeak Notation

Like for **unary verb concepts**, a line representing a **binary verb concept** means nothing more than the verb used in its **wording**. The little directional arrow that appears alongside the line simply indicates how to "read" the verb concept. The proper wording for the verb concept above is therefore understood to be 'plane arrives at [destination] city' — not 'city [destination] arrives at flight' (obviously nonsensical). A starburst is usually omitted for a binary verb concept since what the line represents is generally obvious from the context of the diagram.

Roles are not the usual kind of noun-ish things IT professionals generally expect; that is, they are not 'normal' entity types or classes as understood in data models or class diagrams. Rather, the meaning of these noun concepts is inextricably tied to some verb (e.g., 'arrives at').

Role names are a particularly good way to handle terms that directly reflect the particular choice of verb in the wording of a verb concept. For example, in the following diagram, the role name 'owner' directly reflects the verb of choice, *owns*.

Figure 4–3. Concept model showing a verb-reflecting role name.

Like any other term, a role name is frequently relevant to many kinds of business communication, including statements of business rules. The following sample business rule illustrates.

Business Rule: *A parking citation may be given only to the owner of a vehicle.*

Reversal — Verbs of the Opposite Persuasion

Even if a data model or class diagram gives a verb in one direction of a relationship, it seldom gives it in the opposite direction. Or if it does, it merely offers a preposition. For example, in the following data model, the opposite direction of the verb 'is involved with' is labeled simply 'of'.

Figure 4–4. Data model showing a preposition for the opposite direction of a verb concept.

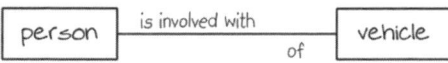

Proper wording for the opposite direction of a verb concept, however, is often needed to express business rules or to compose other kinds of business communication or requirement. The following sample business rule illustrates.

Business Rule: *A vehicle must not <u>transport</u> more than 4 passengers.*

In this business rule, the verb 'transport' is used to clearly express the appropriate meaning. Try substituting 'of' in some way into the statement and see how well that works to express the meaning. (It doesn't.)

In concept modeling, stand-alone prepositions for verb concepts are considered lazyman's verbs. Literally, you can't make complete sentences with only prepositions!

> In concept modeling, stand-alone prepositions for verb concepts are considered lazyman's verbs.

Actually, the communication problem gets even worse. In the real world, people can be involved with vehicles in different ways. 'Passenger' in the business rule above suggests just one way. Suppose that people and vehicles can 'be involved' with each other in at least four ways:

- People own vehicles.
- People lease vehicles.
- People drive vehicles.
- People ride in vehicles.

In data models, such differential 'involvements' are typically handled using a type code treated as 'intersection data'. The following data model illustrates.

Figure 4–5. Data model showing a type code treated as intersection data.

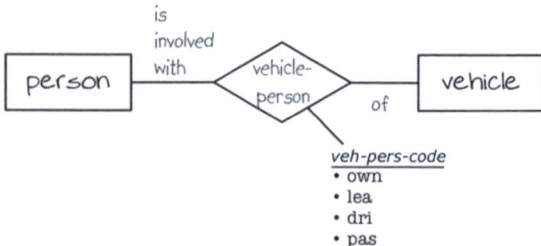

This data model features a new noun-ish thing 'vehicle-person', in which the type code 'veh-pers-code' has been included. Four values of the type code are listed to distinguish the four kinds of 'involvements' from above.

Let's see what now happens to the expression of the passenger business rule. We started with this:

Business Rule: *A vehicle must not transport more than 4 passengers.*

Using the terminology provided by the data model, the rule might now be expressed like this:

Rule: *A vehicle must not be of more than 4 people where veh-pers-code = "pas".*

Do we really want business communications to sound like that?! *No!* The statement contorts the meaning (mangles the **semantics**) almost beyond recognition. Besides losing the clarity of 'transports', we've forced the business people to speak in terms of a type code. That's unnatural. This example clearly illustrates the difference between a true *business* rule (the original version) versus what must be considered a *data* rule or *system* rule (the mangled version).

To emphasize this latter point, let's consider a bit more complicated business rule pertaining to *two* kinds of 'involvements'. First, here is the rule verbalized as a business person might expect:

Business Rule: *A person must not lease a vehicle the person owns.*

Using the vocabulary of the data model above, however, we get the following verbalization:

Rule: *A person must not be involved with the same vehicle where veh-per-code = "lea" and veh-per-code = "own".*

Clearly, the more complicated the business rule, the worse the mangling. And a great many of your business rules are *very* complicated! Without further ado, let's simply agree that's awful and move on. The following diagram indicates how these semantics (verb concepts) would be fully handled in concept modeling.

Figure 4–6. Concept model showing multiple 'involvements'.

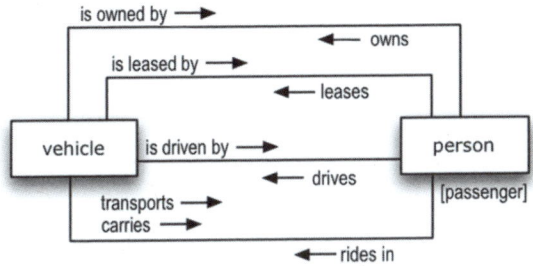

Key observations:

1. Verb concepts are always bi-directional (or multi-directional) even if not worded explicitly in one or more directions. (All the verb concepts above have been worded in both directions for the sake of completeness.) Concept models then are very different from process models, which always designate uni-directional flows.

2. Two or more noun-ish things can be related more than once if the meanings of the verbs are different. Such differentiation has resulted in the four verb concepts above.

3. Any verb concept can have a synonym if the meaning is considered *exactly* the same by the business. In the diagram above, for example, the verbs 'transports' and 'carries' are indicated to be synonyms in the context of the given verb concept.

Now back to the **business rules**. The concept model gives us all the scaffolding we need to verbalize the business rules succinctly and naturally. You can verify that for yourself:

Business Rule: *A vehicle must not <u>transport</u> more than 4 <u>passengers</u>.*

Business Rule: *A person must not <u>lease</u> a vehicle the person <u>owns</u>.*

Using the concept model as a blueprint, we can have a real business conversation with business people and subject matter experts *in natural language* about whether these business rules are valid and complete. Indeed, business analysts should ask some hard questions, including perhaps the following.

- Is the person who *drives* a vehicle considered a passenger?
- Does the business rule also apply to *buses*, or just to passenger cars?
- Does the business rule mean a vehicle can't carry more than 4 passengers *ever*, or just at any given point in time?
- Can the *same* person be a passenger in the *same* vehicle more than one time over time?
- *Why* do we really care how many passengers ride in a vehicle?

The answers to these questions could well indicate that the current concept model is incomplete. For example, if the business rules are from a city government, we might actually want to talk about when to issue *traffic citations*. The actual business rules might be:

> Business Rule: *A passenger overload <u>traffic citation</u> must be written for a passenger vehicle carrying more than 4 passengers.*

> Business Rule: *A <u>traffic citation</u> may be given only to a person driving.*

The noun concept *traffic citation* (and related verb concepts) does not appear in the concept model above. Clearly, some work on that is in store. Now ask yourself this: Would you rather work this out *before* or *after* you get to a data model or class diagram? The answer, I think, speaks for itself.

My point is this. The fundamental problem in business today is not design or implementation of databases or systems. Rather, it is the challenge of business communication. If you can't clearly communicate (verbalize) what you know, you'll never get the database or system you want.

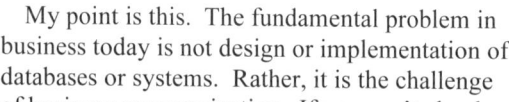
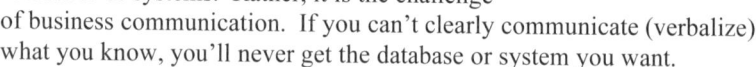

> If you can't clearly communicate (verbalize) what you know, you'll never get the database or system you want.

Where does that take you? Directly to writing complete sentences, which in turn brings you straight to verbs. There's simply nowhere else to turn.

More Ways in Which Concept Models are Verb-ish

Concept models are verb-ish in even more ways than discussed thus far. Two additional areas are examined next.

Objectification

In natural language, we often turn verbs into nouns or noun phrases so we can talk about them as *things*. Doing that is called **nominalization**; often the intent is to objectify the verbs. (The MWUD definition of **objectify** is: [1a] *to cause to become or to assume the character of an object.*) For example, we might objectify the verb concept worded 'person [owner] owns vehicle' into the noun-ish thing *ownership*. The following diagram illustrates, using a dotted line to show that the verb concept has been objectified.

Figure 4–7. Concept model showing objectification.

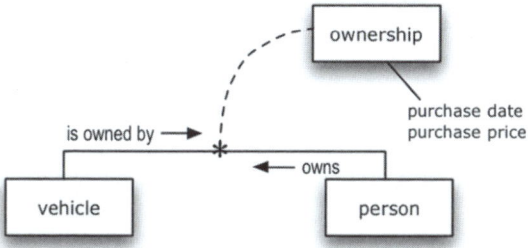

Because **objectifications** (e.g., 'ownership') are things, they can have **properties**. For example, *ownership* might have the following two properties, as illustrated in the diagram.

- *Purchase date* — the date a given vehicle was purchased by a given person.

- *Purchase price* — the price paid for a given vehicle by a given person.

All these terms, including the one given to the objectification, are likely to be relevant to business rules. The following sample business rule illustrates.

Business Rule: *Proof of purchase must be provided to establish ownership of a vehicle.*

States

How do we talk about some potential **state** of something in everyday language? We naturally use a **participle**, generally a **past participle**, another verb construct. The following diagram illustrates informally for the noun concept *order*.

Figure 4–8. Informal representation of states for 'order'.

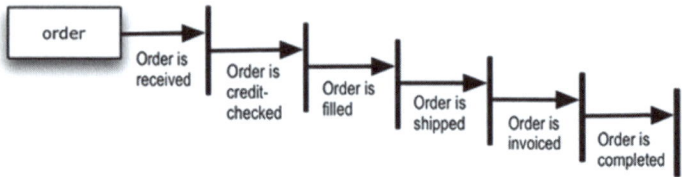

In this example, six states have been identified for the normal life cycle ('happy life') of *order*. Each has been identified using a past participle: *received, credit-checked, filled, shipped, invoiced,* and *completed*. A quick look at the MWUD definitions of 'past participle' and 'participle' puts this usage into perspective. Note especially the words *completed action* — that sense is an important one for business rules, as we'll see momentarily.

> **Past Participle:** *a* **participle** *that typically expresses <u>completed action</u> ...*
>
> **Participle:** *[1]: a word having the characteristics of both verb and adjective; especially: the English verbal adjective ending in -ing or in -ed, -d, -t, -en, or -n*

One especially important use of **unary verb concepts** in concept modeling is to represent states of noun-ish concepts, as the following formalization of the above diagram illustrates.

Figure 4–9. Concept model for the 'happy' states of 'order' using unary verb concepts.

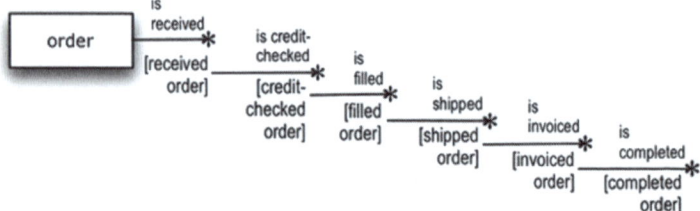

Six unary verb concepts are represented in this diagram. Each unary verb concept is given a **wording** that involves a past participle representing a particular state (completed action) in the life cycle of 'order'. Shown below each unary fact is a name for an order in that particular state:

- A *received order* is an order for which 'order is received' is true.

- A *credit-checked order* is an order for which 'order [received order] is credit-checked' is true.

- A *filled order* is an order for which 'order [credit-checked order] is filled' is true.

- … and so forth.

Note on ConceptSpeak Notation

The particular manner in which the **unary verb concepts** have been specified requires the **states** be strictly cumulative:

- *Credit-checked order* requires that the order 'is [already] received'.

- *Filled order* requires that the order 'is [already] received' *and* 'is [already] credit-checked'.

- *Shipped order* requires that an order 'is [already] received' *and* 'is [already] credit-checked' *and* 'is [already] filled'.

- … and so forth.

Although organizing states to be cumulative like this is not required, it often proves useful.

The resulting state-oriented **vocabulary** for 'order' is a rich (and simple) one for verbalizing business rules — for example:

Business Rule: *A credit-checked order must be verified by at least 3 references.*

Business Rule: *A shipped order must be assigned to a carrier.*

Business Rule: *An expeditor must be assigned to an order shipped but not invoiced for more than a week.*

For an order to attain any given state, it must satisfy all business rules pertaining to that state. To say that differently, think of a state as reflecting a *completed action*. For the action to have been completed successfully, it must have satisfied all relevant business rules. Otherwise, it should fail. The following example illustrates.

Figure 4–10. Concept model showing an 'unhappy' state of 'order'.

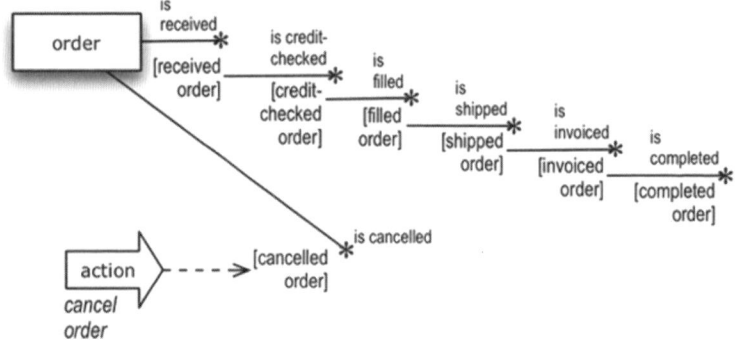

A new unary verb concept worded 'order is cancelled' appears in this diagram. This new verb concept can be used to indicate that an order has been cancelled.

Best Practice

A best practice for modeling **states** is to avoid including 'unhappy' states such as this one within the 'happy life'. Such segregation yields the best results for expressing **business rules**.

Presumably, canceling an order requires some action (or task or process). To illustrate, an action 'cancel order' has been added informally to the diagram. (Actions are not shown in proper concept models.)

The result the action seeks (a cancelled order) can come about only if business rules allow, for example:

Business Rule: *A cancelled order must not have been shipped.*

Under this business rule, the action can achieve the desired state *cancelled order* only if the order has not already been shipped. The state *shipped order* is therefore a **prohibited antecedent**.

A state reflects a completed action. For an action to complete successfully, it must satisfy all relevant business rules.

Note that the business rule is not embedded in the action, but rather has been specified separately. Specification of business rules apart from processes is the essence of **Rule Independence**.

Coming full circle to points made earlier, every verb can be seen from two perspectives — as representing action (processes) or as representing knowledge. Invoking *cancel order*, a process, results in a cancelled order, a bit of knowledge. Business rules fall naturally on the knowledge side. Once you liberate verbs from an exclusive process role, liberating the business rules is the next logical step. And what a powerful thing to do!

Summary

Data models and class diagrams are generally created to serve design purposes. If they include verbs at all, they are not vetted against **business rules** or other forms of operational business communication.

A **concept model**, in contrast, provides the basis for consistent and unambiguous *verbalization* of business rules and other forms of operational knowledge. Verbalization depends on well-constructed sentences, which in turn puts a premium on verbs. As a result, concept models not only address the problem of designing IT artifacts, but the broader problem of business communication.

> A concept model not only addresses the problem of designing IT artifacts, but the broader problem of business communication.

It is time to recognize full-fledged human communication as the starting point for anything textual (verbal) we write about business operations, including business rules and requirements. Concept models provide the necessary scaffolding.

Chapter 5

Creating a Concept Model

How do you create a **concept model**? You start by identifying the basic **terms** of the operational business and defining the **noun concepts** they designate. You build on that by identifying basic **verb concepts**. What does *basic* mean? *Basic* means that a concept cannot be derived or computed from any other, at least not within scope.

You organize the emerging vocabulary as a graphical concept model. Just in case I need to say this: There should be only a single concept model for the entire scope of your effort. The goal is to create a *shared* **business vocabulary**.

In concept modeling, everything eventually comes around to developing good **definitions**, so let's focus on that first.

Forming Definitions

A first principle in defining terms is that any aspect of operational business knowledge that might change over time should be treated as a **business rule**. In forming definitions, therefore, the practitioner should always focus on what is unlikely to ever change — that is, on the fundamental *essence*. (This focus is one of our best practices in **ConceptSpeak**. It is supported, but not necessitated, by **SBVR**.)

> In defining basic concepts, focus on essence.

For example, consider the following definition of *customer* proposed by a practitioner in a real-life project.

Customer: *an organization or individual person that has placed at least one paid order during the previous two years*

Areas of business practice that could change over time are:
- That a customer is *always* an organization or an individual person.
- That *placing orders* is the core criterion for being a customer.
- That a minimum of exactly *one* order is a criterion for being a customer.
- That an order having been *paid* is a criterion for being a customer.
- That the timeframe of exactly *two* years is a criterion for being a customer.

Now consider the MWUD definition of *customer* (2a):

Customer: *one that purchases some commodity or service; especially one that purchases systematically or frequently*

In contrast to the earlier definition, the MWUD version is clearly an *essence definition* and is therefore much better. The embedded business practices of the practitioner's definition should be treated as business rules:

Business Rule: *A customer must be an organization or individual person.*

Business Rule: *A customer has always placed at least one paid order during the previous two years.*

> A business practice subject to change should be treated as a business rule, not embedded in a definition.

You might have noticed the lack of periods at the end of the definitions given above. This omission is intentional, reflecting standard dictionary practice. (Check an authoritative dictionary to confirm that for yourself!) A definition is not a sentence (unless you deliberately make it into one by saying: *An x is a y that...*). See the sidebar below to find out why.

Why No Period at the End of a Definition

A **definition** should be viewed as a phrase or expression that can be substituted for the corresponding **term** in any sentence (e.g., any **business rule** statement) where the term appears, without any change in the meaning of the sentence. Of course, such substitution would often produce very long sentences, but the notion does serve to ensure the fitness (or literally the 'fit') of each definition.

Capturing Verb Concepts and Roles

At its core, a **concept model** is about fundamental connections between **noun concepts**, stripped of quantification and qualification. Consider the business rule from above: *A customer has always placed at least one paid order during the previous two years.* The fundamental connection between the two central noun concepts, 'customer' and 'order', is *places*. The appropriate **wording** for this verb concept is *customer places order*. That really gets down to *barebones* knowledge!

> A concept model represents barebones knowledge.

In arriving at the **verb concept** worded *customer places order*, we stripped away the following:

Quantification: *at least one*

Qualification: *paid*; *during the previous two years*

We also stripped away the articles 'a' and 'the' in the sentence. A wording just gives you the right verb or verb phrase to use for a verb concept; it's a building block for sentences, but never a sentence per se.

> A wording for a verb concept is a building block for sentences.

Graphically, the verb concept can be represented as in Figure 5–1.

Figure 5–1. Graphical representation of a verb concept.

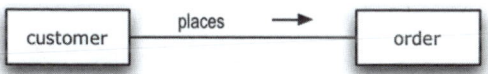

A key question in concept modeling is whether two wordings mean the same thing or something different (i.e., represent the same verb concept or not). Usually, but not always, the answer is obvious. For example, *order is placed by customer* is obviously just a different wording for the verb concept meant by *customer places order*. These two wordings express only one underlying verb concept. Literally, they are two ways to call out the same meaning.

Should the second wording be included in the concept model? In practice, the answer has to do with scaling up. In the early stages of developing a concept model, additional wordings are not usually necessary.

Later on, as the number of business rules grows, additional wordings are unavoidable. For example, consider this new business rule: *A rush order that is placed by a high-risk customer must be paid in advance.* Figure 5–2 illustrates how this second wording should now be included.

Figure 5–2. A verb concept with two wordings.

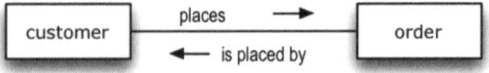

Sometimes, it is not as obvious as in the example that two wordings share the same meaning. Consider *household includes person* and *person belongs to household.* Same meaning? Maybe, although unlike *places* and *is placed by* in the previous example, *includes* and *belongs to* are not merely different forms of the same verb. A practical test would be to ask: Does *person is included in household* always involve exactly the same real-world examples (facts) as *person belongs to household?*

Probably so. The same is also probably true for *household includes person.* So these three wordings probably express a single verb concept.

Assuming that a single verb concept is represented, the wordings should be shown as in Figure 5–3.

Figure 5–3. A verb concept with two wordings that use different verbs.

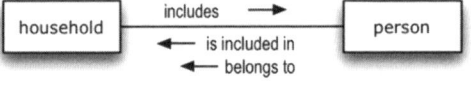

> If two or more wordings share the same meaning,
> they represent just one verb concept.

Business people often have a special term for a noun concept they use only in the context of some particular verb concept. For example, in the verb concept just discussed, business people are likely to say *household includes household member* and *household member belongs to household.* Upon inspection we find that *household member* is simply a more specific term used to refer to a *person* belonging to a household. In other words, the term is a **role**. It can be shown graphically as in Figure 5-4.

Figure 5–4. A role in the context of a verb concept.

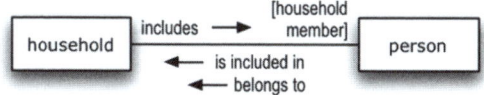

> A role indicates the part a noun concept
> plays in the context of a verb concept.

Note that 'household member' is *not* a synonym of 'person'. To be a synonym, a term must mean *exactly* the same thing as another term. The practical test for *exactly the same thing* is whether each term could be substituted for the other term in *every* sentence (e.g., a business rule statement) where either term appears. That's certainly not the case for *household member* and *person.*

Creating a Concept Model: Case Study

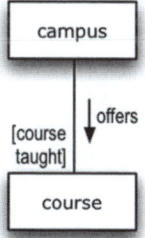

A simple case study illustrates how development of a concept model typically proceeds. Consider a community college that has multiple campuses offering various courses. A first verb concept for their concept model might be worded *campus offers [course taught] course*, as illustrated in Figure 5-5.

Figure 5–5. A first verb concept for the community college concept model.

Both campus and course would probably have properties (e.g., *address* and *date opened* for campus, and *course name* for course), but let's ignore those details and stick to developing core concepts. (More about **properties** in the next Chapter.) A second verb concept for the community college might be worded *student enrolls in campus,* as indicated in Figure 5–6.

Figure 5–6. Adding a second verb concept to the community college concept model.

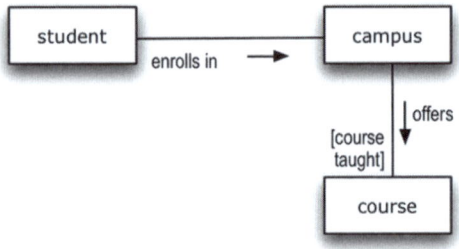

Note that no dependencies are assumed to exist between the two verb concepts; in other words, any specific case of each can stand on its own. By *stand on its own* I mean:

- Any specific case of *campus offers [course taught] course* can exist:
    - *independently* of whether any student enrolls in that campus.
    - *before* any student enrolls in that campus.

- Any specific case of *student enrolls in campus* can exist:
    - *independently* of whether any course is offered by that campus.
    - *before* any course is offered by that campus.

The community college would probably want **business rules** to restrict some of those possibilities. If so, the business rules must be explicit — the concept model doesn't assume them. For example, suppose the community college has a business practice not to enroll students in a campus that does not (yet) offer any courses. (Sounds reasonable!) Such a business practice should be expressed as: *A student may enroll in a campus only if the campus offers some course.*

> A concept model never assumes any business rule.

To continue with the case study, if courses are being offered by a campus, and students are enrolled, the students will naturally want to sign up for courses. For that we need a third verb concept, which can be worded *student signs up for course*. This new verb concept is included in Figure 5–7.

Figure 5–7. Adding a third verb concept to the community college concept model.

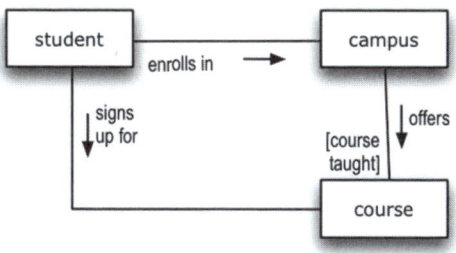

Does the community college permit a student to sign up for a course if the course is not offered at a campus in which the student is enrolled? *Probably not.* Assuming the answer is *no*, the following business rule should be specified: *A student may sign up for a course only if the student is enrolled in a campus that offers the course.*

To continue, the community college would probably want to know some things about a student enrolling at a campus — for example, *when* a given student enrolled in a given campus. How would the **property** *date enrolled* be handled in the concept model?

Date enrolled is not about either a student on his/her own or a campus on its own. Rather, *date enrolled* is about the connection between *student* and *campus* — that is, *date enrolled* pertains to the verb concept worded *student enrolls in campus*. In concept modeling, however, only noun concepts can have properties, not verb concepts. A verb concept is just the meaning of some verb involving noun concepts. It doesn't make sense for a verb concept to have a property. What do we do?

> Verb concepts cannot have properties — only noun concepts can.

To handle *date enrolled* we need to **objectify** the verb concept — that is, turn the verb concept worded *student enrolls in campus* into a noun concept, say *enrollment*. Because enrollment does represent a noun concept, it *can*

have a property. Figure 5–8 shows *enrollment* as an **objectification** of the
verb concept using a dashed line. *Date enrolled*, in turn, is indicated as a
property of *enrollment.*

Figure 5–8. Objectifying a verb concept in the community college concept model.

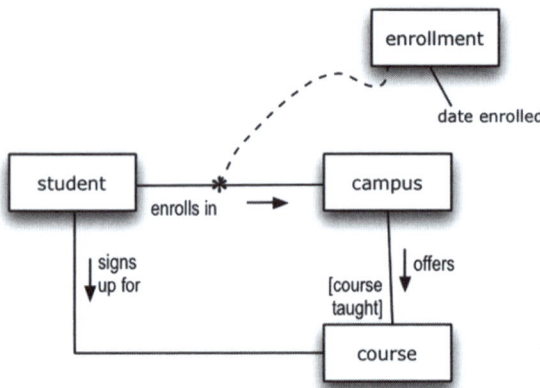

Here's a quick summary of results from our work on the community
college. The concept model currently includes:

- Four basic **noun concepts**, each about a different kind of thing —
  represented by the terms *student*, *campus*, *course*, and *enrollment.*
- Two additional noun concepts — represented by the terms *course
  taught* (the name of a **role**) and *date enrolled* (the name of a
  property).
- Four **verb concepts** worded as follows:
  - *campus offers [course taught] course*
  - *student enrolls in campus*
  - *student signs up for course*
  - *enrollment has date enrolled*
- One **objectification** — the verb concept worded *student enrolls in
  campus* has been objectified as *enrollment.*

Note to the Practitioner

Something this case study does not illustrate very well is the size of a
typical **concept model**, which can easily grow into the dozens or hundreds
of **terms**. To *scale up*, you need an automated tool. Ideal support for
graphical representation includes:

- Faithful coordination with all textual data about the vocabulary
  represented by the concept model.
- Intelligent display across multiple pages or tabs. **ConceptSpeak** calls
  these pages or tabs *neighborhoods.*

Unary, Binary, and N-ary Verb Concepts

Since each of the four verb concepts in the case study involves exactly two noun concepts, each is a **binary verb concept**. The central verb concepts of a concept model are typically binary. Other verb concepts, however, can be **unary** (that is, involve only one noun concept) or **n-ary** (that is, involve more than two noun concepts).

To illustrate, suppose a company builds and markets complex products. Owing to the products' costs and complexity, the company focuses on products being actively marketed. Also, the company's sales representatives often receive special briefings about some specific product by some experienced engineer. At least the following two kinds of knowledge are therefore needed.

- To know whether a product is being actively marketed.

- To know which engineer briefs which sales representative about which product.

Note that the former item refers to only a single noun concept, *product*. The verb concept worded *product is being actively marketed* is therefore *unary*. The second item refers to three: *product, engineer,* and *sales representative*. The verb concept worded *engineer briefs sales representative about product* is therefore *n-ary*. Figure 5–9 illustrates how these two verb concepts can be represented in a concept model.

Figure 5–9. Representing unary and n-ary verb concepts.

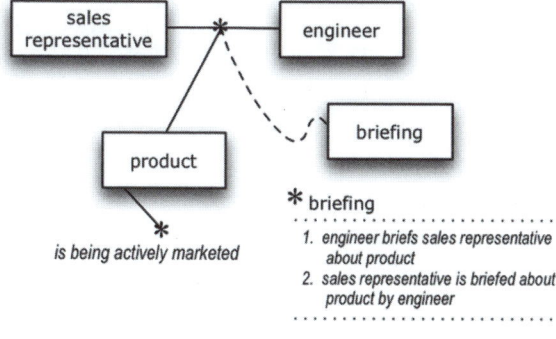

> **Note on ConceptSpeak Notation**
> The asterisk symbol appearing for both **verb concepts** in Figure 5–9 is always used for **unary** and **n-ary** verb concepts. The asterisk is usually omitted for **binary verb concepts**. The asterisk provides a reference point for expressing **wording(s)** for a verb concept. As illustrated by Figure 5–9, a wording for a unary verb concept appears close to an asterisk at the end of a thin line. Wordings for an n-ary verb concept appear in a separate annotation. More about that momentarily.

- A unary verb concept always provides a simple *yes-or-no* answer to some question (i.e., is Boolean). The unary verb concept worded *product is being actively marketed* provides answers to the question, "Is a given product being actively marketed?" Such **state**-related knowledge is often relevant to business rules — for example: *A briefing may be only for a product that is being actively marketed.*

- The n-ary verb concept worded *engineer briefs sales representative about product* cannot be included in the diagram in a practical, unambiguous manner using the three connection lines intersecting at the asterisk. Try it. Note that a second wording is *sales representative is briefed about product by engineer.* That one — and any others — must be worked in too. So these wordings are simply annotated separately from the connection lines.

> **Note on ConceptSpeak Notation**
> The annotation in Figure 5–9 also includes the **term** *briefing* because the **verb concept** has been **objectified**. This **objectification** is represented in the diagram by the box labeled 'briefing', which is connected to an asterisk by a dashed line. The verb concept did not have to be objectified. If it weren't, the term 'briefing' would not have appeared in the separate annotation.

Elementary Verb Concepts

Every verb concept in a graphic concept model should be **elementary**. For each verb concept that includes two or more noun concepts, *elementary* means it should not be possible to break the verb concept down into two or more other verb concepts, each with fewer noun concepts, without losing knowledge.

For example, suppose a briefing were set up to accomplish one or more of the following:

- Cover multiple products.
- Update multiple sales representatives.
- Involve multiple engineers.

In that case, a briefing is not always selective to a particular *combination* of engineer, sales representative, and product. Replacing the n-ary verb concept by two or three individual verb concepts (as appropriate), each involving only two noun concepts, would not lose any selective knowledge. By the way, elementary verb concepts involving three noun concepts, and especially ones with four or more, are *rare* for basic business operations and **know-how**.

> A graphic concept model should include only elementary verb concepts.

A good concept model is a relatively *stable* one with respect to potential changes in business practice. Suppose, for example, that the verb concept worded *engineer briefs sales representative about product* does accurately reflect current business practice. Will that always be the case? Ask: Is there any reasonable chance that in the future the business might want to …

- Set up a briefing that covers multiple products, updates multiple sales representatives, or involves multiple engineers?
- Have the same sales representative briefed about the same product by the same engineer more than one time, over time (and know about it).

The **objectification** can't handle any of those things. An objectification is simply a verb concept directly transformed into a noun concept — never anything more. Remember: No hidden **semantics**!

The safest approach (i.e., the approach most accommodating of future changes) is therefore the following:

- Indicate *briefing* to be a noun concept in its own right, not simply an objectification.

- Include in the concept model three binary verb concepts worded: *briefing is given to sales representative*; *briefing is given by engineer*; and *briefing covers product*.

- Specify one or more business rules if current business practice limits each briefing to just one sales representative, to just one engineer, or to just one product.

In other words, the best approach is to *generalize* the concept model as much as is reasonable, letting business rules handle current and future business practices. The key word in that is *reasonable*. What does *reasonable* mean? *Reasonable* means that there is a chance the business practice will change. If the business practice will assuredly never change, then generalizing the concept model for that possibility is *not* reasonable.

> Generalize the concept model as much as is reasonable;
> handle more restrictive business practices — current
> or future — using business rules.

Summary

In the past, many business people and subject matter experts have been intimidated by data models, class diagrams, and similar IT-centric artifacts. That's unfortunate. A **concept model** should never be viewed as representing anything more than just what it is — a **structured business vocabulary** covering the basic concepts of business operations.

It does take some practice and patience to learn the ropes. After all, a concept model is based on conventions that require discipline.

Beyond that though, understanding a concept model isn't really that hard — *if* you understand the basic knowledge implicit in business operations. The concept model simply makes that basic knowledge explicit. So if a concept model does prove harder to understand than understanding the basic knowledge of business operations, somebody is simply doing something wrong.

Chapter 6

Special-Purpose Elements of Structure

The focus of Chapter 5 was primarily on **verb concepts** whose shape (business meaning) lies completely with the **wordings** supplied for them by business workers and business analysts. Such elements of structure are meaningless without those wordings — they have no implicit or prefabricated meaning of any kind.

Other important elements of structure come in handy, *pre-defined* shapes. This chapter illustrates use of four of these shapes, as presented in Table 6–1. These special-purpose **SBVR** connections between **noun concepts** extend the reach and precision of a **concept model** significantly. Before I get too deeply into that, however, I should give a quick note about the term *instance*.

About the Term *Instance*

At this point in the discussion, I will start taking a few liberties with the **SBVR** concept of **instance**. In SBVR, instances are always in the real world, not in a model. For example, you can't put the real country Canada into a model. Wouldn't exactly fit(!). In a **concept model**, you can include only **concepts** (like the one that stands for Canada).

If you're used to thinking about instances being organized within or by a model (e.g., to be stored in a database), however, that gets a little confusing. So in this discussion, I will use the term *instance* a bit more loosely. Just remember, when business people talk about real-world things, they're *not* talking about instances in some model(!).

Table 6–1. Special-Purpose Elements of Structure.

Special-Purpose Element of Structure	General Form	Example	Use in a Sample Statement
categorization	(Class of thing₁) *is a category of* (class of thing₂).	'Corporate customer' *is a category of* 'customer'.	A customer is always considered corporate if the customer is not an individual person.
property	(thing₁) *has* (thing₂)	order *has* date taken order *has* date promised	An order's date promised must be at least 24 hours after the order's date taken.
composition (whole-part or partitive structure)	(whole) *is composed of* (parts) (part) *is included in* (whole)	chair *is composed of*: • legs • seat • back • armrests	A chair may be ordered without armrests.
classification	(Instance) *is classified as a* (class of thing).	Canada *is classified as a* country. Canadian dollar *is classified as a* currency.	An order may be priced using the currency 'Canadian dollar' only if the customer placing the order is located in Canada.

Categories and Categorizations

A **category** is a class of things whose meaning is more restrictive than, but otherwise compliant with, some other class of things. For example, *male* is a category of *person*. Each male is always a person, but not every person is a male. A male can have **properties** that would not apply to any person who is not a male. In general, a category represents a kind, or variation, within a more general concept.

> A category is a kind, or variation, of a more general concept.

Representing one class of things to be a category of another class of things is called **categorization**. A category is not the same as a **role**; unlike a role, its meaning is not completely tied up in any particular **verb concept**. Figure 6–1 illustrates several categories (using heavy lines) building on the *briefing* example discussed in the previous Chapter.

Figure 6–1. Illustration of categories.

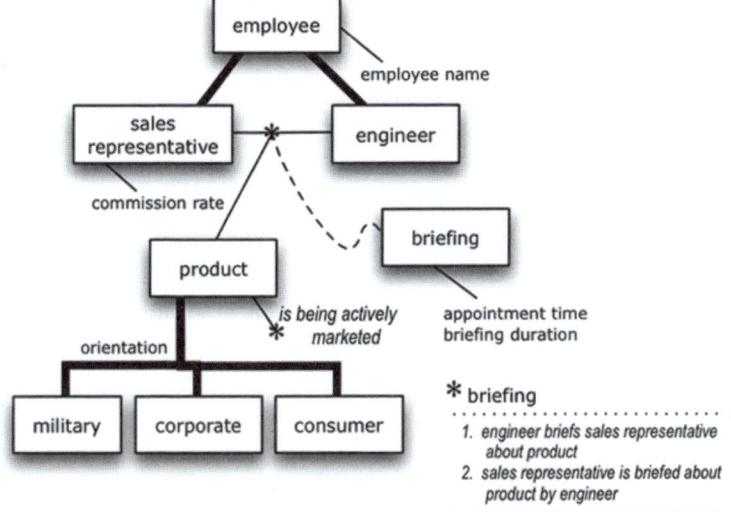

The following *categorizations* are illustrated by Figure 6–1.

- Both *sales representative* and *engineer* are recognized as categories of a more general concept *employee*. Note the property *employee name* is indicated for *employee*. Since all sales representatives and engineers can have names — indeed, *any* employee can — the *name* property is indicated only for *employee*. Remember that all sales representatives and engineers *are* employees in this business, so the *name* property pertains as a matter of course to both *representative* and *engineer*. It does not need to be re-specified for them; applicability (inheritance) of the property is assumed. On the other hand, commission rates apparently pertain only to sales representatives — not to all employees (e.g., not to engineers) — since *commission rate* is indicated only for *sale representative*.

- *Product* now has three categories — *military*, *corporate*, and *consumer* — forming a group. This group of categories is organized on the basis of a **categorization scheme** named *orientation* — more about that later. Note that (as always for categories) *military*, *corporate,* and *consumer* must be products. Indeed, unless everyone reading the diagram is thoroughly familiar with categorization, better labels would probably be *military product*, *corporate product*, and *consumer product*. The boxes represent that anyway, but these revised labels would emphasize the point.

> Be mindful of the more general concept
> in naming or interpreting a category.

Any category can have categories; any category of a category can have categories, and so on. Multiple levels of categorization are not uncommon in concept models. Indeed, such refinement or narrowing of meaning as you go 'deeper' yields a high degree of precision or selectivity for making statements about the business (e.g., expressing **business rules**). For example, a business rule might be expressed for software engineers, a potential category of *engineer*, which does not apply either to other kinds of engineers or to employees in general.

Properties

MWUD defines **property** as *a quality or trait belonging to a person or thing.* Figure 6–1 indicates *employee name* to be a property of *employee*, and *commission rate* to be a property of *sales representative*. A thin line is used to attach each to the appropriate box (noun concept). Exactly what does the thin line represent?

- The thin line does *not* indicate that every member of a class of things actually has an **instance** of the property, only that it *can*. If each member of a class of things must have an instance of the property, an explicit business rule is required (e.g., *An employee must have an employee name.*).

- The thin line is actually shorthand for a **binary verb concept**. The **wording** for this binary verb concept defaults to *(thing₁) has (thing₂)*. The important word here is *has*. The verb *to have* is very general — not specific or descriptive at all. *Has* makes very poor wording for verb concepts not specified as properties. For properties, on the other hand, a *has* default is often convenient.

> A property is a binary verb concept in which one noun concept
> is closely tied to the meaning or understanding of another.

Can properties be worded using verbs other than *has*? *Yes.* For example, the *commission rate* property of *sales representative* might be worded *sales representative is compensated at commission rate*.

The property shown at the end of the line is often actually a role of some other noun concept. For example:

- Suppose commission rates are always percentages (in this business). Then the *commission rate* property of *sales representative* actually represents the verb concept worded *sales representative is compensated at [commission rate] percentage*.

- Similarly, the *employee name* property of employee might actually represent the verb concept worded *employee has [employee name] name*.

Note on ConceptSpeak Notation

Why bother with a graphical shorthand for **properties**? The answer has to do with scaling up. If you were to treat all properties as 'regular' **verb concepts**, the **concept model** would become hopelessly cluttered with connections having to do with such things as numbers, names, dates, units of measure, and much more. Such connections are of secondary importance to the business. Avoid that!

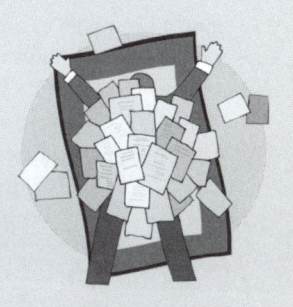

Figure 6–1 actually includes several other properties, as follows.

- Two properties for the **objectification** *briefing* have been indicated using a *single* thin line (another shorthand to reduce clutter).

- *Orientation*, which can be seen just above the crossbar for the categorization of *product*, is also a property, albeit a special kind. *Orientation* is the name of the **categorization scheme** used to organize the three kinds of product. Since *orientation* is a property of *product*, we can say *product has orientation*. (That's like saying *person has gender*, meaning *male* and *female*.) Is it required that every product fall into at least one of the three **categories**: *military, government,* or *consumer*? In other words, must every product have an orientation? (Or perhaps *exactly* one?) Never assume so — that would require some explicit business rule(s).

Compositions — Whole-Part (Partitive) Structures

Many things in the real world are composites, made up of several other kinds of thing. For example, an automobile (simplistically) is composed

of an engine, a body, and wheels. A mechanical pencil is made up of a barrel, a lead-advance mechanism, pencil lead, and eraser (from [ISO 704 2000], p. 9). An address (simplistically) is made up of a street number, a street, an apartment number, a city, a state/province, a country, and a zip code / postal code.

Sorting out the terminology and composition of such **whole-part structures** is often quite useful. Before looking at a graphical example, let's address some relevant questions:

- Is every **instance** of the whole in a whole-part structure required to have at least one instance of each part? *No.* For example, not every address has an apartment number. If every instance of the whole *is* required to have some part(s), an explicit business rule must be given.

- Can an instance of a whole have more than one instance of a kind of part? *Yes.* An automobile must have at least three wheels (a business rule). But use caution here. A whole-part structure usually works best where there is only one, or a small number of, each part.

- Can the specification of a whole-part structure indicate only one kind of part? *Yes.* However, exercise common sense! For example, is it really useful to consider the **verb concept** worded *order includes line item* to be a whole-part structure? We do not favor that practice.

- Can a part itself be a whole composed of other parts? *Yes.* Multiple levels of composition are possible.

- Can both the whole and the parts be selectively involved in verb concepts on their own? *Yes.*

- Can an instance of a part exist independently from an instance of the whole? *Yes* (unless business rules disallow it). A wheel, for example, can be removed from an automobile.

- Can an instance of a part be in more than one instance of a whole at the same time? *Yes* (again, unless business rules disallow it). A power source, for example, can be part of more than one circuit.

> A whole-part structure permits
> capture of terms involved in composition.

Figure 6–2 illustrates a composition of *briefing* using a tree structure of thin lines to indicate the parts. The **wording** for this **verb concept**, not shown explicitly, is assumed to be: *briefing is composed of: introduction, main body, conclusion.* (Or, as they sometimes say in the military, *tell 'em what you're gonna to tell 'em, tell 'em, and tell 'em what you told 'em.*)

Figure 6–2. Example of a composition (whole-part structure).

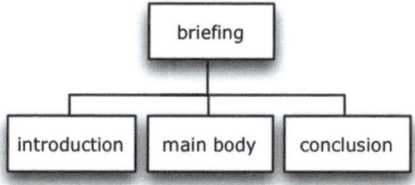

Classifications

A central focus in concept modeling is on identifying, defining, and naming the classes of things important to basic business operations. Most often the business cannot possibly know in advance what all the **instances** will be of a class of things. For example, most businesses cannot predict all their future customers.

For certain classes of things, however, the business can identify or prescribe in advance some or all of the instances, especially for those classes where the instances are relatively stable. For example, we know all the European countries at the present time. Moreover, the business will need to pre-define instances when it has some business rule(s) that pertain selectively to them — for example: *A shipment may be made only to the European countries United Kingdom or The Netherlands.*

Representing the connection between an instance and its particular class of things is called **classification**. Figure 6-3 illustrates. The line with the double-wavy hatch mark indicates a classification connection from the class of things *European country* to some of its instances.

Note on ConceptSpeak Notation
The double-wavy hatch mark indicates that a meta level is crossed. To avoid clutter, we recommend ample use of neighborhoods to depict **instance**-level terminology.

Figure 6–3. Example of classification.

United Kingdom
The Netherlands
Germany
Italy
Switzerland

Some additional examples of classifications:

- *Health care:* All recognized health services — e.g., *consultation, office visit, hospital admission, surgery,* and so on.

- *Ship inspection:* All recognized parts of a ship — e.g., *bulkhead, hatch cover, railing, deck,* and so on.

These examples were chosen deliberately to illustrate that classifications can be multi-level. For example, the instances *bulkhead, hatch cover,* etc. of the class of things *ship part type* might themselves be viewed as classes of things with respect to *specific* bulkheads, hatch covers, etc. These specific bulkheads, hatch covers, etc. probably have serial numbers and would be found on a given ship or in a given shipyard. Business rules might be targeted toward any of these levels.

> A classification permits capture of an instance-level term.

Summary

Certain elements of structure useful for concept modeling come in handy, pre-defined shapes. This chapter has illustrated four of these special-purpose elements of structure: **properties**, **categorizations**, **compositions**, and **classifications**. These special connections between noun concepts extend the reach and precision of the **concept model** significantly. They also allow statements to be written with great precision — for example, giving **business rules**. Let's turn now to that.

Part 3

Business Rules

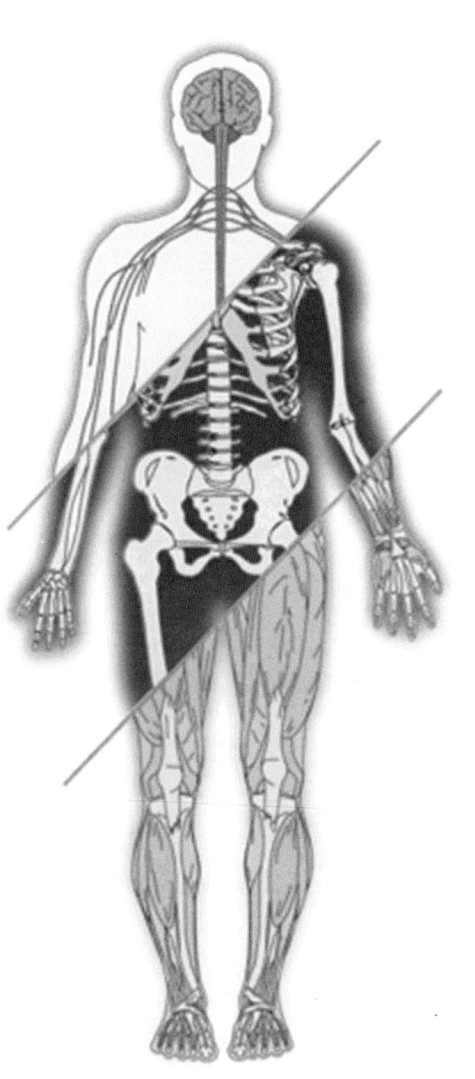

Chapter 7

Business Rules

Business rules apply to a broad spectrum of needs. To illustrate, consider the following situation that might occur in a baseball game. Suppose it's the bottom of the seventh inning, with two outs, two strikes on the batter, and two base runners. The score is tied. The batter is left-handed.

- One business rule might ensure the batter still gets only three strikes even if the pitcher is changed.
- Another business rule (or set of business rules) might compute the batter's hit percentage in similar prior circumstances.
- Yet another set of business rules might help choose the best relief pitcher.

Business rules cover all such needs, and more — all the kinds of guidance needed for business operations. Understanding these kinds of guidance is a 'must' for business analysts.

Fortunately, business rules fall into fundamental categories. In surveying those categories, we will also look at non-rules (advices), guidelines, exceptions, and more. A reminder — this treatment of business rules is based on, and consistent with, **SBVR**.

What is a Business Rule?

A **business rule** is simply a rule that is under business jurisdiction. **Under business jurisdiction** is taken to mean that the business can enact, revise, and discontinue their business rules as they see fit. If a rule is not under business jurisdiction in that sense, then it is not a business rule. For example, the 'law' of gravity is obviously not a business rule. Neither are the 'rules' of mathematics.

> A business rule is simply a rule
> under business jurisdiction.

The more basic question is the real-world, non-IT meaning of **rule**. Clearly, *rule* carries the sense of *guide for conduct or action* both in everyday life and in business. One way or another, this sense of *rule* can be found in most, if not all, authoritative dictionaries.

> A real-world rule serves as a guide for conduct or action.

If a rule is to serve as a guide for conduct or action, it must also provide the actual criteria for judging or evaluating that conduct or action. In other words, a rule serves as a *criterion* for making judgments and **decisions**. A business definition of *rule* therefore encompasses the sense of *criteria* as given by authoritative dictionaries.

> A real-world rule serves as a criterion
> for making judgments and decisions.

A rule always tends to remove a degree of freedom. If there were no rules, there would be complete freedom — a.k.a. anarchy. If some guidance is given but does not tend to remove some degree of freedom, it still might be useful, but it is not a rule per se. Such guidance is called an **advice**.

Figure 7–1 presents an overall categorization of guidance from the perspective of business people. All rules are either **behavioral** (also called *operative*) or **definitional** (also called *structural*). Use Figure 7–1 as a reference for the rest of this Chapter.

> A real-world rule always tends to remove a degree of freedom.

Figure 7–1. Categorization of business guidance.

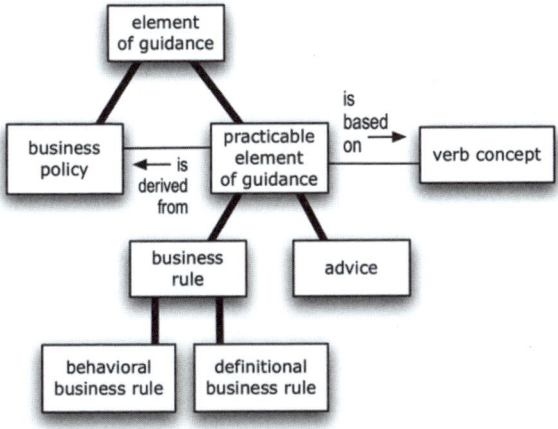

In contrast to a *business policy*, a business rule needs to be **practicable**. This means that a person who knows about a business rule could observe a relevant situation including his or her own behavior and decide directly whether or not the business was complying with the business rule.

In general, a **business policy** is not practicable in that sense; a business policy must be interpreted into some more concrete business rule(s) that satisfy its supposed intent. (That's what the verb concept in Figure 7–1 worded *practicable element of guidance is derived from business policy* is about.) For example the following business policy is not practicable: *Safety is our first concern.*

A business rule must be practicable.

Just because business rules are practicable does *not* imply they are always automatable — many are *not*. For instance, consider the business rule: *A hard hat must be worn in a construction site.* Such a non-automatable rule needs to be supported as a **role** responsibility of some worker(s) or by some **procedure(s)**. In many ways, managing non-automatable rules is even more difficult than managing automatable ones. They definitely have a place in your **rulebook**.

> Non-automatable rules should be managed too.

For a business rule (or an advice) to be practicable assumes that the business vocabulary on which it is based has been adequately developed, and has been made available as appropriate. Note the verb concept in Figure 7-1 worded *practicable element of guidance is based on verb concept*. Every business rule (and advice) should be directly based on a **structured business vocabulary**. Each business rule (and advice) is expressed using **terms** and **wordings** to create statements in building-block fashion.

Meaning vs. Statement
An additional, subtle point is this. The statement of a **business rule** is not actually the business rule; the *meaning* of the statement is the business rule. That's important because:

- The very same business rule (or advice) can be expressed by statements in different languages — e.g., French, Mandarin, etc. (It's a global world these days!)

- Even in the same language and the same notation (e.g., **RuleSpeak**), it's not uncommon to find a business rule (or advice) expressed in different ways by different people. That's a kind of redundancy you need to be able to discover and sort out.

In short, managing business rules needs to be about managing meaning — **semantics** — not just statements.

Behavioral Rules

Consider the business rule expressed as: *A gold customer must be allowed access to the warehouse.* Let's assume for now we don't need to consider any exceptions. Clearly this business rule can be violated. If a gold customer is denied access to the warehouse, then a **violation** has occurred. Presumably, some sanction is associated with such violation — for example, the security guard might be called on the carpet.

Any business rule that can be violated *directly* is a **behavioral rule**. (It doesn't matter whether it is automatable or not.) Behavioral rules are really *people* rules. Basic business operations typically involve significant numbers of behavioral rules.

> A business rule that can be violated directly is a behavioral rule.

Behavioral rules always carry the sense of *obligation* or *prohibition*. To reflect that sense, **RuleSpeak** prescribes the rule keywords *must* or *only* to express behavioral rules.

One way or another, behavioral business rules are always preventative, as the following examples illustrate.

- *Surgical gloves must be worn in performing surgery.*
  This business rule is intended to prevent infections.

- *A nurse must visit a patient at least every 2 hours.*
  This business rule is intended to prevent inattention to patients.

- *A gold customer must be allowed access to the warehouse.*
  This business rule is intended to prevent any denial of access.

 Behavioral rules (also called **operative rules**) enable the business to run (i.e., to *operate*) its activities in a manner deemed suitable, optimal, or best aligned with its goals. Behavioral rules deliberately preclude specific possibilities (of *operation*) that are deemed undesirable, less effective, or potentially harmful. Behavioral rules remove those degrees of freedom. Often, sanction is real and immediate if a behavioral rule is broken.

Although the examples of behavioral rules above are not automatable, many can be automated. Here are some examples:

- *An order over $1,000 must not be accepted on credit without a credit check.*

- *A high-risk customer must not place a rush order.*

- *An order's date promised must be at least 24 hours after the order's date taken.*

Not Automatable?
Be careful about assuming a business rule can't be automated in some way. Sometimes, given the right technology (and sufficient business motivation) you might be surprised. Consider the business rule discussed earlier: *A person must wear a hard hat in a construction site.* You could use something like facial recognition software to determine whether a person is wearing a hardhat. If a person is not wearing one, the response could be to lock a gate the person needs to pass through or to trigger an alarm. Or put a GPS device on both the person and the hat. Don't underestimate technology!

Behavioral rules — *people rules* — are a distinctive feature of the business rules paradigm. All behavioral rules are business rules — people rules are always **under business jurisdiction**.

You may have noted that none of the examples of business rule statements given above (or anywhere in this book) use *if-then* syntax. A major reason is that if-then syntax is not well-suited for expressing behavioral rules. See sidebar for explanation.

Why Not *If-Then*?

Consider the **business rule** statement: *An employee must have a name.* What is the *then* of that? From a business perspective there is no *then*. There might be some enforcement if the rule is violated, but that's a different matter.

A typical IT counterpart might be: *If an employee does not have a name, then [do something].* The focus of this specification is not to express the rule, but rather to look for **violations** and do something in response. That focus is off-target for the primary business need.

In good English construction, every sentence has a subject. Although this subject may be implied or the sentence inverted, more often than not an explicit subject appears as the first word or phrase in the main body of the sentence. Such sentences are usually direct, and if well written, easy to follow. (The subject in the previous sentence, for example, is 'sentences'.)

So **RuleSpeak** does not use if-then syntax. It prescribes that statements of guidance always have an explicit subject at the beginning. That subject should be a noun, possibly qualified.

For additional discussion, see [Ross 2007].

Behavioral rules have fundamental implications in several areas:

- **Reasoning.** Since behavioral rules can be broken, they require special care in reasoning (automated or otherwise). Consider the behavioral rule: *A gold customer must be allowed access to the warehouse.* It cannot be assumed that the business rule has always been faithfully enforced; therefore, it cannot be inferred that in every situation where it was appropriate for a gold customer to be allowed access to the warehouse, the customer actually *was* allowed such access. Violations happen. Reasoning must be carefully restricted in this regard for behavioral rules.

- **Processes.** Business rules have significant (and perhaps surprising) consequences for modeling processes. A key question in that regard is how the business *selectively* responds to **breaches** of any particular business rule (if at all). That question, in turn, raises the issue of how strictly each behavioral rule should be enforced — that is, its appropriate **enforcement level**. I'll save that discussion for Chapter 12.

Definitional Rules

Additional business rules would be relevant to evaluating the behavioral rule: *A gold customer must be allowed access to the warehouse.* Specifically, what criteria should be used for determining whether a particular customer is *gold* or not? Here is an example: *A customer is always considered a gold customer if the customer places more than 12 orders during a calendar year.*

Such business rules are called **definitional rules**. Definitional rules always carry the sense of *necessity* or *impossibility*. To reflect that sense, **RuleSpeak** offers the alternate rule keywords *always* or *never* to express a definitional rule.

Note to the Practitioner
Examples of definitional rules in this chapter and elsewhere in the book use the keywords *always* or *never* (or permissible variations) for clarity and emphasis. In current practice, distinguishing **behavioral** vs. **definitional** rules via selective keywords is not the greatest concern. For practical guidelines, refer to www.RuleSpeak.com.

Let's return to our two business rules. Suppose a customer appears at the warehouse, but the security guard is unaware of the criteria expressed in the definitional rule, or misapplies that criteria. Quite possibly the customer will not be given due access. The error, however, manifests itself as a violation of the behavioral rule, *not* the definitional rule per se. Definitional rules can be ill-conceived, misunderstood, or misapplied, but they cannot be directly violated.

> A definitional business rule can be ill-conceived, misunderstood, or misapplied, but it cannot be violated directly.

Unlike behavioral rules, not all definitional rules are business rules. The reason is that not all definitional rules are **under business jurisdiction**. As mentioned earlier, the 'law' of gravity is obviously not under business jurisdiction. Neither are the 'rules' of mathematics.

Evaluation of a *definitional rule* always classifies or computes something. For example:

Classification Rule: *A customer is always considered a gold customer if the customer places more than 12 orders during a calendar year.*

Given any customer, evaluation of this definitional rule indicates whether the customer is or is not *gold* given everything known about that customer (roughly, all relevant facts).

> Computation Rule: *The total price of an order item is always computed as the product unit price times its quantity.*

Given any order item, evaluation of this definitional rule indicates the one result for *total price* that the known facts justify.

During business operations, definitional rules are used to evaluate 'where you are' — that is, the current state of affairs — as the need arises. For example:

- Is this customer a gold customer or not?
- Do we owe this customer a discount on this order?
- Does this patient have cat scratch fever or something else?

The result reached in each case is only as good as the logic given by the business rules. Poor or misapplied guidance yields poor or inconsistent results. In that case, some aspect of the knowledge 'breaks down' — it simply does not work properly.

Behavioral rules and definitional rules are fundamentally different. Disregard for behavioral rules leads to violations and possible sanctions; misapplication of definitional rules leads to miscalculations and off-base conclusions — but only indirectly, if at all, to violations.

If you are concerned about violations, you always need a behavioral rule. Consider the example of a definitional rule given earlier: *The total price of*

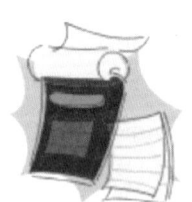

an order item is always computed as the product unit price times its quantity. Suppose a salesman decides to give a special volume discount to a personal friend. Again, the original business rule is merely for calculation; it does not prohibit inappropriate conduct. For that, you would need a separate behavioral rule — for example: *A special volume discount may be given only to high-volume customers.*

For sets of definitional rules, you will often want to understand how their evaluation reaches particular results. More about that in the sidebar.

> Definitional rules are about how you organize — that is,
> *structure* — basic knowledge.

> **Logic Traces**
> Accurately evaluating (i.e., *reasoning over*) large numbers of **definitional rules** (automated or not) can produce unexpected or non-intuitive results. Often, the end-user or business analyst will want to ascertain *how* the results were produced — that is, to audit the way the logic was applied. Doing that requires starting with the results and tracing back through the chain of rules that led to the results.
>
> Automated support for such *logic traces* is an important platform capability. A logic trace permits flaws and opportunities for improvement in logic to be identified. It also provides a means for less knowledgeable workers to learn about business **know-how** in hands-on fashion.

Definitional rules (also called **structural rules**) are about how the business organizes (i.e., *structures*) its basic knowledge. They give shape — i.e., *structure* — to core **concepts** of the business.

> A behavioral rule shapes business conduct;
> a definitional rule shapes business knowledge.

More Things You Should Know

Definitional Rules and Definitions

Definitional rules clearly contribute to the meaning of concepts. Obviously **definitions** do as well. In practice, can a clear distinction be maintained between definitions and definitional rules?

Yes. As discussed in Chapter 4, a good definition focuses on the essence of a **concept** — the core meaning of the concept to the business. Definitional rules, in contrast, indicate the exact lines of demarcation — that is, the precise 'edges' of the concept. Establishing these lines of demarcation are how definitional rules remove degrees of freedom.

For example, consider an 'essence' definition of *gold customer:* a customer that does a significant amount of business over a sustained period of time. Now compare that with the associated definitional rule: *A customer is always considered a gold customer if the customer places more than 12 orders during a calendar year.*

The definition expresses the fundamental notion about what *gold customer* means to the business or, more precisely, to business *people*. It is unlikely that basic notion will change — in other words, the notion as defined is very stable. That stability helps maintain continuity of knowledge within a community over time. It also aids in training newcomers, as well as in communicating with people outside the business area. In short, definitions should be aimed at *people*.

Note to the Practitioner
Aiming definitions toward people is our recommended best practice. It is supported but not required by **SBVR**.

The definitional rule, in contrast, gives precise criteria for determining whether a customer is or is not *gold* — criteria that quite possibly will change over time. Any aspect of business practice subject to change should be treated as a business rule, not embedded in definitions.

> Definitions are for people.

Another difference between definitions and definitional rules is that the latter frequently provide criteria that would not be so obvious from the definition, for example: *A customer is never considered a gold customer if the customer has been incorporated less than a year.*

Non-Rules (Advices)

Consider the statement: *A bank account may be held by a person of any age.* Although the statement certainly gives business guidance, it does not directly:

- Place any obligation or prohibition on business conduct. Therefore it does not express a behavioral rule.

- Establish any necessity or impossibility for knowledge about business operations. Therefore it does not express a definitional rule.

Because the statement removes no degree of freedom, it does not express a rule. Rather, it expresses something that is a non-rule — a.k.a. an **advice**.

Is it important then to write the advice down (i.e., capture and manage it)? *Maybe.* Suppose the statement reflects the final resolution of a long-standing debate in the company about how old a person must be to hold a bank account. Some say 21, others 18, some 12, and some say there should be no age restriction at all. Finally the issue is resolved in favor of no age restriction. It's definitely worth writing that down!

> An advice emphasizes what is possible or permissible
> as a matter of current business policy.

Now consider this statement: *An order $1,000 or less may be accepted on credit without a credit check.* This statement of advice is different. It suggests a business rule that possibly hasn't been captured yet: *An order over $1,000 must not be accepted on credit without a credit check.* Let's

assume the business needs this rule and considers it valid.

In that case you should write the *business rule* down — not the advice — because only the business rule actually removes any degree of freedom. Just because the advice says an order $1,000 or less may be accepted on credit without a credit check, that does not necessarily mean an order over $1,000 *must not.* A statement of advice only says just what it says.

Guidelines

Consider the behavioral rule: 'An order over $1,000 must not be accepted on credit without a credit check.' Suppose this behavioral rule is restated with a *should* instead of a *must* such that it reads: 'An order over $1,000 should not be accepted on credit without a credit check.' Now does it express an advice?

No. It is still a business rule, only with a lighter sense of prohibition. What actually changed was its presumed **enforcement level**. Rather than strictly enforced, now the business rule has the sense: *It's a good thing to try to do this, but if you can't there's no sanction.* In other words, now it's simply a **guideline** (or *suggestion*, if you prefer).

> A guideline is a behavioral rule with no tangible enforcement.

Should you use *should* or *should not* (or similar forms) to express a lightly-enforced behavioral rule? *Not recommended.* In general, it's better to use consistent wording for all behavioral rules (e.g., *must* or *must not*). Remember, the enforcement level for any given business rule often varies with changes in business practice. Guidance is one thing; enforcement is another — best not to mix the two! By the way, that's why you don't find *guideline* in Figure 7–1.

Two other things about guidelines:

- **Vocabulary.** A guideline for business operations — just like an advice or any other business rule for the same business — is expressed using the same underlying **vocabulary**. Note that in Figure 7–1 *all* elements of guidance *are based on* verb concepts. Let's put it this way: If you have the vocabulary to express your business rules, you already have the vocabulary you need to express any guideline.

- **Guidance Message.** Recall from Chapter 2 that a business rule statement *is* a **guidance message**. This remains true for guidelines. A guideline can indeed be violated, but no enforcement action is taken. Instead, the end user (if authorized) is simply informed. If you think of business rules simply as hard-and-fast constraints, you're missing an important part of the picture. In the larger sense, business rules are always about dispensing basic business knowledge in real time. Guidelines are an important part of that overall scheme.

Exceptions

No discussion of business rules would be complete without considering **exceptions**. To do the topic justice, however, requires a bit of groundwork. Let's examine the following two warehouse business rules:

Business Rule 1: *A gold customer must be allowed access to the warehouse.*

Business Rule 2: *A customer may have access to the warehouse only during regular business hours.*

Suppose some *gold* customer seeks access *after* regular business hours. Under that potential **scenario** we have a **conflict**.

A basic **SBVR** principle is that any guidance statement whose meaning conflicts with some other guidance statement(s) (or even some other part of the same statement) must be taken that way. In other words, if by taking some expression(s) literally you find that a potential conflict could arise, you are right — it can. You need to fix it. The principle is really about being able to fully trust what you read in front of you. If statements of business rules don't mean *literally* what they say, then can you really ever be sure what they do say!?

> You have to be able to trust
> what a statement of a business rule says.

So guidance statements should always be taken to mean exactly what they actually say — no more, no less. Potential conflicts such as the above must be resolved explicitly, within the actual statement(s). Several approaches that *don't* work in that regard include:

- Setting up some priority scheme to determine which 'wins'.
- Expressing some separate business rule(s) to determine which 'wins'.
- Deferring to some level of **categorization** to determine which 'wins' (e.g., A gold customer is a **category** of customer; therefore 'customer' rules 'win' over 'gold customer' rules).

To apply each business rule correctly under any of these approaches, sometimes you need to know more than just what a statement says. In other words, sometimes **semantics** are hidden, or at least external. Not good.

> If you understand the business vocabulary,
> you should never have to know more than exactly what a
> guidance statement says to fully understand it.

The only viable solution is that once a potential conflict is discovered, the guidance statement(s) that produce(s) that conflict need to be restated to avoid it. In other words, the statement(s) must *accommodate* the problematic circumstances. This **SBVR** guiding principle — the correct one for business communication — is called *Accommodation*.

So one of the warehouse business rules needs to be re-written. Which one? The answer depends entirely on business practice. Which of the following reworded versions might represent the correct or desired business practice?

> Reworded Business Rule 1: *A customer must be given access to the warehouse if the customer is a gold customer and the access is during business hours.*

> Reworded Business Rule 2: *A customer that is not a gold customer may have access to the warehouse only during business hours.*

Let's say the desired business practice is given by the second statement. So the two business rules jointly representing the correct business practices for warehouse access are:

> Business Rule 1: *A gold customer must be allowed access to the warehouse.*

> Business Rule 2: *A customer that is not a gold customer may have access to the warehouse only during business hours.*

Now we can finally address the issue of exceptions. Looking at the two resulting warehouse-access business rules ask yourself: *Which is an exception?!* Both? Neither? The formal answer is, once you *accommodate*, there really are no exceptions(!). There are just well-stated, fully-trustworthy business rules.

In conversation and other informal business communication, we often do talk about "exceptions" to business rules. For example we might say: *A customer may have access to the warehouse only during regular business hours.* Then later in the same conversation or message we might add: *By the way, none of what I've said applies to gold customers.*

Statements of business rules, however, should not be informal in that sense. You can never be sure when or where a statement might be read or what the context might be. So a business rule statement needs to express its full meaning. David Crystal, a noted world authority on language, explains things this way [Crystal 2005, p. 465]:

> "When someone consults a reference book … [in which] information is stored for future use, it is impossible to predict who is likely to use it … There is no 'dialogue' element in the communication. The information has to be as self-contained as possible, for it is impossible to predict the demands which may one day be made on it, and in most cases there is no

way in which the user can respond so as to influence the writer. Accordingly, when language is used for [such] purposes … it is very different from that used in everyday conversation — in particular, it displays a much greater degree of organization, impersonality, and explicitness."

Now I've never met or talked to David Crystal, but I'm confident I get his meaning.

> A business rule statement needs to express its full meaning.
> This principle is called *Wholeness*.

This **SBVR** principle of expressing the full meaning of each business rule is called *Wholeness*. Suppose your **rulebook** is deemed free of conflicts and you understand the business vocabulary correctly (two big *ifs* of course). If your guidance statements are all expressed *wholly*, then:

- *Every statement is always self-explanatory.* No need to appeal to any other statement should ever arise in understanding the full meaning.

- *Every statement can always be taken at face value.* Take it out of conversational context and you can still trust exactly what it says.

By the way, there's a great deal a **general rulebook system (GRBS)** could do to simplify and condense *whole* statements for easier consumption — *if* it knew each worker's preferred conversational context. That would give you friendly *and* formal business communication.

> What you ultimately want is
> *friendly-and-formal* business communication.

Summary

Rule Independence is the key idea in **business rules**. The various principles underlying Rule Independence are enumerated in the *Business Rules Manifesto*, a copy of which can be found at the end of this book.

One consequence of Rule Independence is that business rules become an object of study and expertise in their own right — a new and exciting competency. The focus of that competency should be strongly centered on the perspective of business people.

There is still more to come. The next step is to fully appreciate how business rules relate to events. Let's now turn to that important topic.

Chapter 8

Business Rules and Events: Flash Points

Intuitively, we know that certain **business rules** apply when certain events occur. But how exactly?

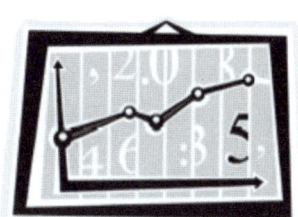

At the risk of stating the obvious, let me begin by clarifying that a business rule and an event are not the same thing. There should be no confusion about that. A business rule gives guidance; an **event** is *something that happens* (MWUD – *event* 1a).

Multiple Events for Each Business Rule

How do business rules and events relate? Consider the business rule: *A customer must be assigned to an agent if the customer has placed an order.* Figure 8–1 shows the relevant **terms** and **wordings** for this business rule statement.

Figure 8–1. Terms and Wordings for the Agent-Assignment Business Rule.

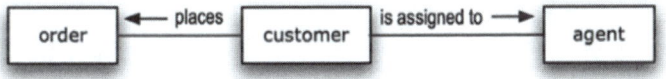

The business rule itself has been expressed in **declarative** manner. This means, in part, that it does not indicate any particular process, **procedure**, or other means to enforce or apply it. It is simply a business rule — nothing more, nothing less.

Declarative also means that the business rule makes no reference to any event where it potentially could be violated or needs to be evaluated. The business rule does not say, for example, "*When* a customer places an order, then...."

This observation is extremely important for the following reason. "*When a customer places an order*" *is not the only event when the business rule could potentially be violated.* Actually, there is another event when this business rule could be violated: "*When* an agent leaves our company...." This other event could pose a **violation** of the business rule under the following circumstances: (a) The agent is assigned to a customer, and (b) that customer has placed at least one order.

In other words, the business rule could potentially be violated during *two* quite distinct kinds of events.

- *When* a customer places an order ...
- *When* an agent leaves our company ...

The first is rather obvious. The second is much less so. Both events are nonetheless important because either could produce a violation of the business rule.

This example is not atypical or unusual in any way. In general, *every* business rule (expressed in declarative form) produces two or more kinds of events where it could potentially be violated or needs to be evaluated. (I mean *produces* in the sense of *can be analyzed to discover*.)

We call these events **flash points**. Business rules do exist that are specific to an individual event (more on that momentarily), but they represent the exception, not the general case.

> A business rule generally produces two or more
> events — *flash points* — where it needs to be evaluated.

Let's summarize what I've said so far:

- Business rules and events, while related, are not the same.

- Specifying business rules declaratively helps ensure no flash point is missed.

- Any given business rule, especially a **behavioral rule**, needs to be evaluated for potentially multiple flash points. Figures 8–2 and 8–3 provide additional examples to reinforce this crucial insight.

Figure 8–2. Multiple Events for a Simple Business Rule.

Business Rule: *A customer must have an address.*

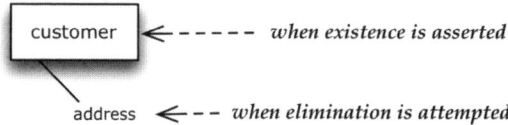

Flash Points:

Event #1: *When an attempt occurs to assert the existence of a new customer.*

Event #2: *When an attempt occurs to eliminate the address of a customer.*

Figure 8–3. Multiple Events for a More Complex Business Rule.

Business Rule: *A territory must not include more than one of the following:*
* Non-candidate traditional gas station,
* Ultra-service,
* Food outlet.

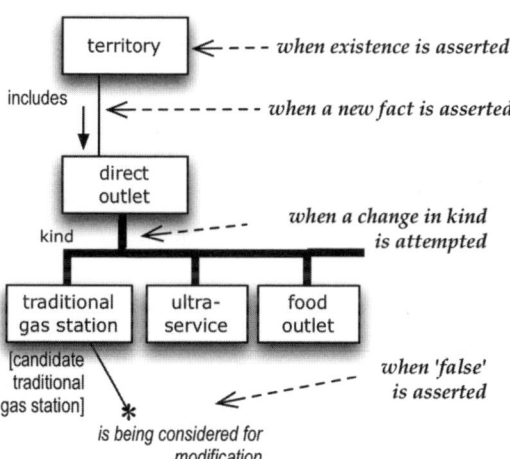

Flash Points:

Event #1: *When an attempt occurs to assert the existence of a new territory.*

Event #2: *When an attempt occurs to include a direct outlet in a territory.*

Event #3: *When an attempt occurs to change the kind of a direct outlet already included in a territory.*

Event #4: *When an attempt occurs to assert that a traditional gas station already included in a territory is not being considered for modification.*

Why is that insight so important? *The two or more events where a business rule needs to be evaluated are likely to occur within at least two, and possibly many, different processes, procedures, or use cases.* Yet for all these different processes, procedures, and use cases, there is only a *single* business rule. By specifying the business rule only once, and faithfully supporting all its flash points wherever they occur, you ensure consistency across all the processes, procedures, and use cases.

> By faithfully supporting all flash points for a business rule
> wherever they occur, you ensure consistency
> across all processes, procedures, and use cases.

Discovering and analyzing flash points for business rules often also proves a very useful activity in validating business rules. Important and sometimes surprising guidance issues (a.k.a. **business policy** questions) often crop up. This capability is one of many for **validation** and **verification** of business rules that a **general rulebook system (GRBS)** can and should support.

> Your general rulebook system (GRBS) should
> automatically identify all flash points
> for each business rule as part of validation.

This type of business-rule-centric event analysis is not a feature of *any* traditional requirements or IT methodology. Once you fully appreciate that point, you can begin to see why legacy systems so often produce such inconsistent results.

CRUD Events

CRUD stands for create, retrieve, update, delete — all *system* events. You should never express business rules based on CRUD. For one thing, CRUD isn't business terminology so the result will always be a data or system rule rather than a business rule. Not good!

But there's more. Using CRUD to express rules has hidden side effects. Often the result is an unintended or unknowing limiting of coverage to a single event. Let's work through an example:

> **CRUD Rule:** *Update product cost if the cost of any of the product's components changes.*

In **RuleSpeak**, the subject of any computation rule is always the name of what is being computed. *Product's cost* is therefore indicated as the subject in the following revised version.

> **Business Rule:** *A product's cost must be computed as the sum of the cost of all the product's components.*

The original CRUD version for this business rule limits coverage to a single flash point — *when* the cost of a component included in a product changes. The revised version covers not only that flash point, but the following two as well:

- *When* a component is newly added to the make-up of a product.
- *When* a component is newly removed from the make-up of a product.

This broadening of coverage should be analyzed carefully, of course — it might not represent true business intent. (If not, the appropriate *when* clause should appear explicitly in the **RuleSpeak** version. By convention the clause should appear at the end, not the beginning, of the statement.) My point is this: CRUD is simply a *when* condition in technical garb. *No when condition, especially a disguised one, should ever appear in a business rule statement accidentally.*

> No *when* condition should ever appear
> in a business rule statement accidentally.

Let's consider another example:

> **CRUD Rule:** *Don't delete a customer that has placed any open orders.*

What is the true business intent of this rule? It stands to reason that if deleting a customer that has placed an open order is disallowed, then *opening* an order *without* a customer is probably also disallowed. From a business perspective, always knowing who the customer is for any open order would be essential. Removing the CRUD produces:

> **Business Rule:** *An open order must be placed by a customer.*

This revised version omits any mention of the *delete a customer* flash point. It inherently also covers the *open an order* flash point (i.e., asserting that an order is open). Even this simplest possible business rule turns out to have more than one flash point!

In **RuleSpeak**, *when* is always taken to mean *only at the point in time that some specified event occurs*. Suppose the rule above had been written as follows (not recommended because of the CRUD word *created*):

> **Rule:** *An order must have a promised shipment date <u>when</u> the order is created.*

In this version, the rule applies only *when* an order is created (comes into existence). But what about two seconds later?! Should anybody (or any system) be allowed to delete (eliminate) the promised shipment date? *Probably not!*

Including a *when* clause in the expression of a business rule chains the business rule to that specific flash point. More often than not, that narrowing of coverage does not reflect true business intent. Experience has shown that the large majority of business rules are inherently and naturally multi-flash-point. Be very careful when you say *when*!

> Including a <u>when</u> clause in the expression of a business rule chains it to that specific flash point.

Summary

The large majority of **business rules** have multiple **flash points** — **events** when they need to be evaluated. These flash points are inherent to any business rule expressed **declaratively**. No flash point should ever be mentioned in stating a business rule unless first verified as specifically expressing business intent.

Separation of business rules from events, another aspect of **Rule Independence**, has many benefits including:

Agility: Each business rule can be specified declaratively and *in one place*. One-place specification (**single-sourcing**) means the business rule will be easier to find — and easier to change quickly.

Consistency: Unification of each business rule across all its flash points ensures consistency across all processes that produce those events. Better for the processes; better for the business rules!

Chapter 9

The Art of Business Rules

A consequence of **Rule Independence** is that **business rules** become an object of analysis and expertise in their own right — a new and exciting business competency. Several key skills are needed for that new competency.

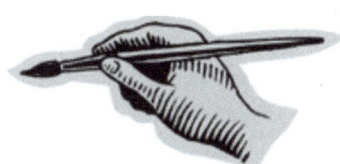

Drilling Down

When business rules are first captured, they often embed multiple criteria that need to be broken out as separate business rules. Breaking them out is called *drilling down*. The goal is to produce easily-understood, highly-granular expressions of business guidance that can be independently re-used and modified.

> *Drilling down* on business rules produces easily-understood, highly-granular expressions of business guidance that can be independently re-used and modified.

To briefly illustrate, consider the following computation business rule:

Starting-Point Business Rule: *The total price of an order item is always computed as the product unit price times its quantity minus 10% if the order is the first order ever placed by the customer.*

To reduce complexity, a good first step is to break out any computations as separate business rules. As a result:

> Business Rule 1 (Definitional): *The first-time discount is always computed as 10% times the total price of an order item.*

Be alert for any more general concept(s) not mentioned by the original statement that might apply. For example, the first-time discount is perhaps just one of many discounts that sometimes might be *applicable* to order items. As a result:

> Business Rule 2 (Definitional): *The first-time discount is always considered an applicable discount for each order item of the first order that a customer places.*

Restate the starting-point business rule using the new **term** *applicable discount*. The result is always a simpler statement:

> Business Rule 3 (Definitional): *The total price of an order item is always computed as the product unit price times its quantity, minus applicable discounts.*

Quality Assessment

Determining the quality of business rules — their *fitness* — is not an IT issue; it's a business one. You want to ensure quality *before* business rules are translated into any implementation language or deployed into actual business operations. Your worst-case scenario is tripping over **anomalies** live! The earlier you detect them, the better (and the cheaper!). The goal is to pursue quality for business rules directly and proactively.

> The earlier you detect anomalies in business rules,
> the better — and the cheaper!

Assessing the quality of business rules falls into two general areas: *validation* and *verification*.

Validation means ensuring the correctness of business rules with respect to business purpose. You want to make certain that, when applied, the results will be appropriate in all relevant circumstances. Validation is largely a matter of human inspection, but a **general rulebook system (GRBS)** can assist in certain ways:

- Diagrams can depict logical or computational dependencies between business rules.

- Test **scenarios** can be retained so prior results can be compared with new results for modified rule sets.
- Each business rule can be analyzed to identify all **flash points**, to help ensure its logic is complete and robust.

> Rule validation is about whether
> you have the *right* business rules.

Verification means assessing fitness with respect to logical consistency. Verification involves discovering business rules (usually two or more in combination) that exhibit some anomaly. Below is a quick sampler of common anomalies, along with simple examples. Can you figure out what's going on in each case?

Linguistic Equivalence
- *A permanent employee must receive a salary.*
- *An employee who is permanent must receive a salary.*

Modal Equivalence
- *An order over $1,000 must not be accepted on credit without a credit check.*
- *An order over $1,000 may be accepted on credit only with a credit check.*

Logical Equivalence
- *A high-risk customer must not place a rush order.*
- *A rush order must not be placed by a high-risk customer.*

Subsumption
- *A rush order must have a destination.*
- *An order must have a destination.*

Outright Conflict
- *A high-priced, fragile item must be picked up by the customer.*
- *A high-priced, fragile item must be shipped by an insured carrier.*

Unintentional Block-Out
- *A shipment must include more than 1 order.*
- *An out-of-state shipment may include only 1 order.*

> Rule verification is about whether your business rules are *right*.

Business rules will be captured by different people at different points in time, so anomalies can appear even in the best-coordinated efforts. By the way, such anomalies are not the result of **Rule Independence**; legacy systems have always been rife with anomalies. Rather, independent expression of business rules in **declarative** form simply makes the anomalies much easier (and cheaper) to find.

Fortunately, detection of many anomalies can be automated. There is only one caveat, but it's a big one: *You must coordinate the* **business vocabulary** *used to express the business rules.*

> Your general rulebook system (GRBS) should provide analysis tools directly supporting quality assessment of business rules.

An additional area of concern in quality assessment for business rules is the *completeness* of business rules — that is, whether there are gaps or holes in coverage. As a simple example, consider this statement of **advice**: *An order $1,000 or less may be accepted on credit without a credit check.* A missing business rule might be: *An order over $1,000 must not be accepted on credit without a credit check.*

Decision Tables

As you scale up, having an effective means to visualize and manage entire *sets* of business rules at a time becomes ever more important. **Decision tables** are an excellent tool for that. In general, decision tables can be used where three criteria are met. These sound more difficult than they really are.

1. A significant number of rules are parallel — that is, they share the same subject, have exactly the same **consideration(s)** (evaluation term(s)), and are equivalent (but not identical) in effect. In other words, the business rules all share a common pattern and purpose.

2. Each consideration has a finite number of relevant **cases (instances** or collections of instances). Collections of instances are usually represented as ranges of values — a.k.a. *brackets*.

3. Given the different cases for the considerations(s), the **outcomes** cannot be predicted by a single formula. (If a single formula could predict the outcomes, using a single business rule or set of business rules to give the unified formula is a better approach.)

> Decision tables represent sets of business rules.

Here is a simple example involving eight business rules:

1. Applicable sales tax is to be 6.0% if year = 2008.
2. Applicable sales tax is to be 6.5% if year = 2009.
3. Applicable sales tax is to be 6.5% if year = 2010.
4. Applicable sales tax is to be 6.5% if year = 2011.
5. Applicable sales tax is to be 6.25% if year = 2012.
6. Applicable sales tax is to be 7.0% if year = 2013.
7. Applicable sales tax is to be 8.0% if year = 2014.
8. Applicable sales tax is to be 8.15% if year = 2015.

Note that this set of business rules satisfies all three criteria above:

1. The eight business rules are exactly parallel. They share the same subject, *applicable sales tax*; have exactly the same consideration, *year*; and are equivalent (but not identical) in effect, an indicated *sales tax percentage* for each given year.

2. The consideration, *year*, has a finite number of relevant cases (eight).

3. The outcomes — the percentages indicated for *applicable sales tax* — cannot be predicted by a formula.

> **Decision tables are an excellent means
> to visualize and manage parallel business rules.**

The following decision table and associated business rule statement show the consolidated decision logic for the eight business rules above.
I think you'll agree it's quite an improvement!

Business Rule:
*Applicable sales tax is to be the
percent value in the Sales Tax
by Year Table for a given year.*

Sales Tax by Year Table

Year	Applicable Sales Tax
2008	6.0
2009	6.5
2010	6.5
2011	6.5
2012	6.25
2013	7.0
2014	8.0
2015	8.15

Decision tables are also useful for finding missing business rules — that is, for assessing the *completeness* of a set of business rules. For example, if any cell in a decision table has nothing in it, that outcome is possibly missing and probably should be addressed. I'll return to the issue of completeness later.

The decision table above has only a single consideration. Most decision tables have more than that. To illustrate, the following decision table adds a second consideration *county* to determine *applicable sales tax*. The decision table uses an intersection format, a natural one for business people, to support the two considerations.

Business Rule: *Applicable sales tax is to be the percentage in the Sales Tax by Year and County Table for a given year and county.*

Sales Tax by Year and County Table

Year	County			
	Harkin	*Lopes*	*Qwan*	*Quail*
2008	6.95	8.2	7.35	4.0
2009	6.73	8.3	9.0	4.5
2010	6.15	8.4	9.0	5.0
2011	6.15	8.3	9.0	5.5
2012	6.15	8.4	6.75	6.0
2013	6.15	8.2	6.75	6.75
2014	5.75	8.2	6.75	7.0
2015	5.95	8.4	7.5	7.25

Representing *more* than two considerations using an intersection format can become problematic. The decision logic can still be represented in variations of the intersection format, however, if no more than three or four considerations are simple (have only two or three cases each). An example of *simple* is the consideration *Is income taxable?* which can be answered by only *yes* or *no*. Such variations might use:

- Split rows or columns within a single table.

- Multiple tables, with one table per relevant case of one (or more) of the considerations. (Think tax tables.)

If some decision logic is based on more than three or four **simple considerations**, an alternative format for the decision table must unfortunately be used. (Automated support by a **general rulebook system (GRBS)** or other tool becomes indispensable too.) The following decision table illustrates.

Business Rule: *The delivery method for an order is to be as in the Delivery Method Table.*

Delivery Method Table

Delivery Method for an Order

Considerations	picked up by customer	shipped by normal service	shipped by premium service
rush order	no	yes	yes
order includes fragile item	no	yes	—
order includes specialty item	no	no	—
order includes high-priced item	no	no	—
order includes item involving hazardous materials	no	yes	yes
category of customer	silver	gold	platinum
destination of order	—	local	remote

The Delivery Method Table establishes the basis for determining the appropriate delivery method for an order. Seven simple considerations appear in the leftmost column as labels for the rows. Six of the considerations are binary (*yes, no* or *local, remote*), whereas one, *category of customer*, involves three cases (*silver, gold, platinum*).

The appropriate choice of a delivery method for an order (shown at the top of the other columns) depends on what appears in all the cells of a column. A dash (—) in a cell indicates that the associated consideration does not matter in determining the outcome; that is, *any* case for that consideration will produce the same outcome.

> Special analyses can be performed
> automatically for decision tables to ensure
> quality and completeness.

Decision tables with more than three or four simple considerations are unavoidably complex, so they must be developed with special care. As always, the issue of completeness is also important. How complete is the sample decision table above? *Not very!* Can you tell why? The answer is worked out on the next page.

Answer to the Delivery Method Table Completeness Question

The completeness of the **decision table** can be calculated as follows:

(1) The total number of *possible* combinations for **cases** of the seven **considerations** can be calculated as: $2^6 \times 3 = 192$. This calculation reflects the fact that six of the considerations apparently have two cases each (*yes* and *no* for five of them, and *local* and *remote* for the other), whereas the seventh (category of customer) apparently has three (*silver*, *gold*, and *platinum*).

(2) The total number of combinations *actually represented* in the decision table can be determined as follows. Column 2 represents one combination — each cell has something in it. Columns 1 and 3 are a bit more complicated because they both have one or more cells with dashes, indicating acceptance of any valid case — for example, either *yes* or *no*. Column 1 includes one such cell, so that column actually provides the basis for establishing the **outcome** for *two* combinations — one if the cell had *local* and one if it had *remote*. Column 3 includes three such cells, so that column actually establishes the basis for 2^3 or 8 outcomes. Altogether, the decision table establishes outcomes for 11 combinations $(2 + 1 + 8 = 11)$.

(3) Having determined how many combinations the decision table actually addresses (11), we can now determine how many it does not: $192 - 11 = 181$. So some 181 possible combinations have not been addressed at all! We must therefore conclude this decision table is *not very complete*.

Summary

A consequence of **Rule Independence** is that **business rules** become an object of analysis and expertise in their own right — a new and exciting business competency. This chapter briefly surveyed three key skills needed for that new competency: *drilling down, quality assessment,* and **decision tables**.

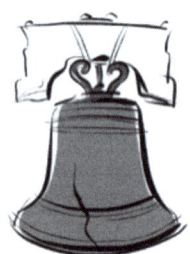

Part 4

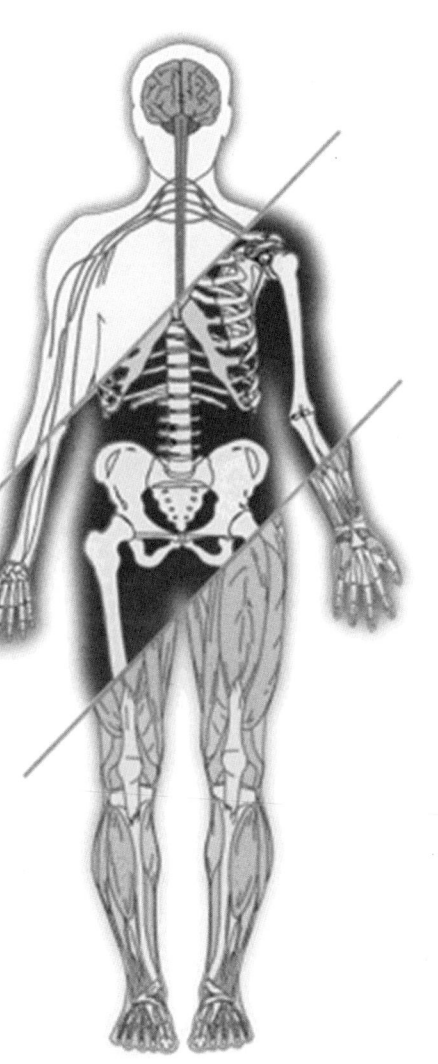

Architecture

Chapter 10

Smart Architectures and the Point of Knowledge

Let's stand back and take a look at some very big questions. What do **business rules** offer business architecture? How should you think about **business vocabularies** (**semantics**) and business rules in the context of enterprise architectures and software design? Where do you want your company to be headed in retaining, managing, and deploying its fundamental **know-how**? How do you get your company to the *point of knowledge*?

When you start to fully understand business rules, a whole lot of other pieces of the puzzle fall right into place. You arrive at **smart architectures**, which gives you *smart knowledge management* and *smart processes*.

The Point of Knowledge

For me, the **point of knowledge (POK)** is a real place. POK is where elements of operational business know-how — business rules — are developed, applied, assessed, re-used, and ultimately retired. In other words, POK is where business rules happen. Knowledge is power, so you can also think about POK as point of *empowerment*.

> The point of knowledge is a real place.

POK corresponds to point of sale (POS) in the world of commerce. POK and POS are similar in several ways:

- In both, something is exchanged. In POS, it's goods. In POK, it's operational business know-how (from here on I'll just say *know-how*).

- In the world of commerce, we often say that consumer and supplier are *parties* in point-of-sale events. Each of us is a consumer in some point-of-sale events, and many of us act as suppliers in others. The same is true for POK. Each of us is a consumer of know-how in some POK events, and many of us act as suppliers in others. Sometimes we switch **roles** within minutes or even seconds.

- A well-engineered experience at the point of sale has obvious benefits both for the consumer — a positive buying experience — and for the business of the supplier — real-time intelligence about sales volume, cash flow, buying trends, inventory depletion, consumer profiles, etc. A well-engineered experience at the POK likewise has obvious benefits. For the consumer, it means a positive *learning* experience. For the business of the supplier, the benefits include real-time intelligence about the 'hit' rate of business rules, patterns of evolving consumer (and supplier) behavior, emergence of compliance risks, etc.

> A well-engineered POK produces a positive learning experience for consumers of operational business know-how.

The consumer/supplier experience at the POK is crucial to worker productivity and job satisfaction. In no small measure, optimizing this experience is the real challenge in POK engineering. It must be deliberate. After all, what's exchanged at the POK is know-how — something you can't carry around in your hands.

> What's exchanged at the POK is know-how — something you can't carry around in your hands.

Nonetheless, your company's know-how is very real. What do I mean by *know-how*? MWUD says:

know-how: *accumulated practical skill or expertness ... especially: technical knowledge, ability, skill, or expertness of this sort*

Today, much of your know-how is tacit — lose the people, you lose the know-how they carry in their heads. How can you avoid that? Make the know-how *explicit* as business rules. That's what POK are about.

Critical success factors in engineering an effective POK include:

- Communication must be strictly in the language of the business, not IT.

- Interaction must be gauged to the knowledge level (and authorization) of each individual party.

- Less-experienced parties playing the consumer role must be enabled to perform as closely as possible to the level of the company's most experienced workers.

- Know-how — business rules — must be presented and applied in a succinct, highly-selective fashion.

- Know-how — business rules — must be presented and applied in a *timely* fashion (i.e., 'just-in-time') to accommodate fast-paced refinement and change in **business policies** and practices.

Point-of-Knowledge Architecture

Let me use an example to sketch the workings of business rules in smart architecture. Refer to Figure 10–1 to visualize how the system works.

Figure 10–1. Point of Knowledge Architecture (POKA).

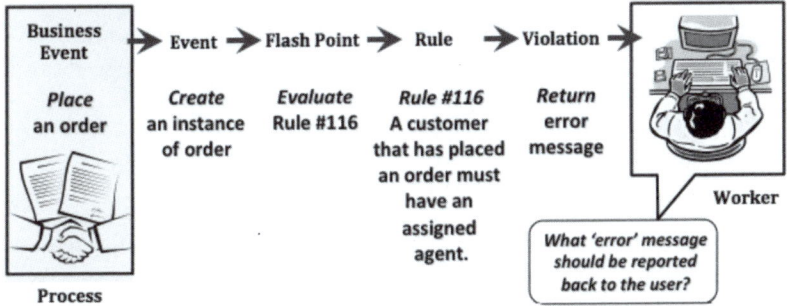

Suppose you have a process or **procedure** that can be performed to take a customer order.

- An order is received. Some kind of event occurs in the system. It doesn't really matter too much what kind of event this is; let's just say the system becomes aware of the new order.

- The event is a **flash point** — one or more business rules pertain to it. One is: *A customer that has placed an order must have an assigned agent.*

- We want **real-time compliance** with business policy, so this business rule is evaluated immediately for the order. Again, it doesn't much matter what component in the system does this evaluation; let's just say some component, service, or platform can do it.

- Suppose the customer placing the order does *not* have an assigned agent. The system should detect a fault, a **violation** of the business rule. In other words, the system should become aware that the business rule is not satisfied by this new state of affairs.

- The system should respond immediately to the fault. In lieu of any smarter response, at the very least it should respond with an appropriate message to someone, perhaps to the order-taker (assuming that worker is authorized and capable).

What exactly should the error message say?

Obviously, the message can include all sorts of 'help'. But the most important thing it should say is what kind of fault has occurred from the business perspective. So it could start off by *literally* saying, *"A customer that has placed an order must have an assigned agent."* We say the business rule statement *is* an **error message** (or better, a **guidance message**).

That's a system putting on a smart face, a knowledge-friendly face, at the very point of knowledge. But it's a two-way street. By flashing business rules in real-time, you have an environment perfectly suited to rapidly identifying opportunities to evolve and improve business practices. The know-how gets meaningful mindshare. That's a ticket to continuous improvement and true business agility.

> Smart architecture offers continuous opportunities
> to evolve and improve business rules.

Smarter and Smarter Responses

Is it enough for the system simply to return a guidance message and stop there? Can't it do more? *Of course.*

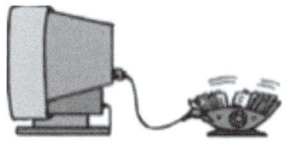

For the order-taking **scenario**, a friendly system would immediately offer the user a means to correct the fault (again assuming the user is authorized and capable). Specifically, the system should offer the user another procedure, pulled up instantaneously, to assign an appropriate agent. If successful, the user could then move on with processing the order.

This smart approach knits procedures together just-in-time based on the flash points of business rules. It dynamically supports highly-variable patterns of work, always giving pinpoint responses to **business events** (not system events). In short, it's exactly the right approach for process models any time that applying know-how is key — which these days, is just about always!

> Smart architecture knits procedures together just-in-time
> based on the flash points of business rules.

The *Business Rules Manifesto* says this: "Rules define the boundary between acceptable and unacceptable business activity." If you want

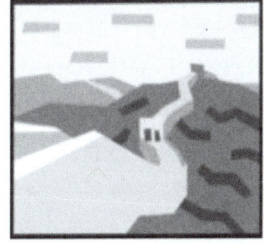

dynamic processes, you must know exactly where that boundary lies, and how to respond to **breaches** (at flash points) in real time.

Is that as smart as processes can get? Not yet. Over time, the business rules for assigning appropriate agents might become well enough understood to be captured and made available to the system. Then when a fault occurs, the system can evaluate the business rules to assign an agent automatically. At that point, all this **decision-**

making gets tucked very neatly under the covers. Even if the business rules you can capture are sufficient for only routine assignments, you're still way ahead in the game.

Smart architecture based on business rules is unsurpassed for **incremental design**, where improvement:

- Focuses on real business know-how, not just better GUIs or dialogs.

- Continues vigorously after deployment, not just during development.

- Occurs at a natural business pace, not constrained to software release cycles.

The *Manifesto* says it this way: "An effective system can be based on a small number of rules. Additional, more discriminating rules can be subsequently added, so that over time the system becomes smarter." That's exactly what you need for knowledge retention, as well as to move pragmatically toward the knowledge economy. Business rules give you *true* agility.

> A smart architecture based on business rules
> is unsurpassed for incremental design.

Smarter and Smarter Workers

Now let's talk about smart architecture from a consumer point of view. What people-challenges face your business today? What role should business systems play?

Time shock. As the rate of change accelerates, workers are constantly thrust into new **roles** and responsibilities. They must be guided through unfamiliar procedures and know-how as thoroughly and as efficiently as possible. The business pays a price, either directly or indirectly, if getting workers up to speed is

too slow (or too painful). Time shock is like culture shock — very disorienting if you're not prepared for rapid immersion.

> Time shock is like culture shock — very disorienting
> if you're not prepared for rapid immersion.

Training. The flip side of time shock is training — *how* to get workers up to speed. Training is expensive and time-consuming. Yet as the rate of change accelerates, more and more (re)training is required. Where do you turn for solutions?

The foremost cause of time shock for business workers is rapid change in the business rules. At any given time, workers might be found at virtually any stage of time shock. Sometimes, you might find them completely up-to-speed, other times completely lost. Most of the time, they are probably somewhere in between. That poses a big challenge with respect to training.

The only approach to training that will truly scale is on-the-job self-training. That requires smart architecture, where pinpoint know-how can be put right in front of workers in real time as the need arises — that is, right at the point of knowledge. What that means, in effect, is that the relevant portion of the company's know-how — its **rulebook** — is 'read' to the worker on-line, right as the worker bumps up against the business rules.

So a key idea that business rules bring to architecture is that operational business systems become *knowledge companions* for workers in the knowledge economy. After all, isn't making *people* smarter the whole point of knowledge?!

> Operational business systems must become knowledge
> companions for workers in the knowledge economy.

Summary

The **point of knowledge** is a real place. **POK** is where **know-how** — **business rules** — are developed, applied, assessed, re-used, and ultimately retired. In other words, POK is where business rules happen.

   In **smart architecture**, business systems become knowledge companions, enabling never-ending, on-the-job training. **Flash points** of knowledge — real-time evaluation of business rules — enables dynamic processes and personalized, just-in-time delivery of up-to-date guidance.

A smart architecture is one equipped to address the formidable challenges facing businesses today — the accelerating rate of change, massive customization, and products and services that are ever richer in knowledge. Effective engineering of the POK is the new litmus test for agility.

> Effective engineering of the POK is
> the new litmus test for agility.

Chapter 11

Business Rules and Business Processes

Many companies today are looking to manage business activity on more of a beginning-to-end, value-add basis. That requires thinking cross-organizationally and developing business process models, always keeping to the business perspective. Can business rules help? Yes, *hugely*.

How Business Rules Relate to Business Processes

Just in case I need to say this, yes, you still need business process models when you do **business rules**. Business rules do not substitute for business processes, they just make them a lot better.

The best definition of **business process** I have found to date is Janey Conkey Frazier's: *the tasks required for an enterprise to satisfy a planned response to a business event from beginning to end with a focus on the roles of actors, rather than the actors' day-to-day job.*

What do business rules do for business processes? Roger Burlton says it this way: "If you separate the business rules, you can develop remarkably stable business processes." If you're looking to manage business activities on a business-process basis, stability is key. Burlton goes on to say: "The really rapid change is in the business rules ... *not* in the business processes." *Right!*

> The really rapid change is in the business rules, *not* the business processes.

How do business rules and business processes relate? Burlton observes that business processes "… transform inputs into outputs *according to guidance* — policies, standards, rules, etc.…." The key phrase in that is *according to guidance*. Guidance is exactly what business rules provide.

Perhaps the most serious mistake people make in modeling business processes is including series of binary evaluation points ('diamonds') where flows branch based on *yes-or-no* (Boolean) logic. What's wrong with that?

For one thing, many *business* **decisions** (most?) aren't binary(!). For another, the business process model quickly becomes so detailed and cluttered, you lose sight of the business value-add. Good communication and business buy-in fade fast.

Quite simply what people are often trying to do when they embed a series of diamonds in their business process models is to represent the logic of business rules **procedurally**. Burlton characterizes that practice this way: "Anytime you stick diamonds in your business process model you're dead." Call it a *worst* practice.

> Sticking diamonds in your business process model
> is a *worst* practice.

Definitional Rules and Business Processes

The relationship of **definitional rules** and business processes is a direct one. Definitional rules simply off-load work pertaining to knowledge. They do so in two basic ways:

Computation: Computation rules provide logic needed to perform calculations.

Derivation: Derivation rules provide logic needed to determine whether or not something is true. See sidebar.

About Derivation, Classification, and Decisions

Determining whether something is true or not means deciding whether something does or does not fall into some particular class of things — that is, classification. For example, does this patient have cat scratch fever? In other words, does this patient's **case** fall into the cat-scratch-fever class of things? As this example illustrates, derivation rules are directly relevant to the general problem of making determinations — i.e., **decisions**.

For either computation or derivation, logic can become quite complex involving many business rules. Trying to capture all those business rules within the 'flow' of a business process model is *utterly hopeless*.

> Trying to capture business rules within the 'flow'
> of a business process model is hopeless.

Instead, definitional rules should be externalized, and referenced or invoked indirectly. That can occur in several ways:

- *Via an input or output specified for a task.* For example, an input to the task "Charge customer" might be *total price of an order item.* This input can be computed using the definitional rule *The total price of an order item is always computed as the product unit price times its quantity, minus applicable discounts.*

- *Via the name of a task.* For example, in insurance you might see a decision task called 'Adjudicate Claim'. This task requires a decision to be made, which in turn requires definitional rules (probably a great many).

- *Via the expression of a conditional flow.* For example, in insurance you might see conditional flows such as 'if claim complete' or 'if fraud suspected'. These conditions indicate determinations to be made; again definitional rules are required.

Behavioral Rules and Business Processes

Behavioral rules are ones that *people* could violate were they to undertake some action. In a game of football, behavioral rules are why you need referees on the field during each game — someone to watch and intervene if any **violations** occur. Behavioral rules arise any time people could be involved in a business process (not just knowledge).

> Behavioral rules arise any time
> people could be involved in a business process.

Behavioral rules generally pertain to compliance of all kinds. A business process can involve hundreds of behavioral rules (or more!) each addressing some specific point(s) of compliance with **business policy** or other **governing rules**. For example: *A customer that has placed an order must have an assigned agent.*

Behavioral rules also address certain flow-related issues quite familiar to those creating business process models. Two of these issues, iteration and service level agreements, are discussed briefly below.

Iteration. Business process models often include loops that permit iteration. Timing and repetition criteria for these loops can be expressed as business rules, for example:

Maximum time allowed between iterations.

> Behavioral Rule: *Additional information needed for a claim must be requested at least every 5 days if not received.*

Minimum time allowed between iterations.

> Behavioral Rule: *Additional information needed for a claim must not be requested more often than every 24 hours.*

Maximum iterations permitted.

> Behavioral Rule: *The total number of requests made for additional information needed for a claim must not exceed 10.*

Maximum time permitted for completion.

> Behavioral Rule: *A request for additional information needed for a claim must not be made after 10 days.*

Service Level Agreements. A service level agreement generally involves four things: (1) an action item, (2) a party, (3) escalation criteria, and (4) timing criteria.

> Behavioral Rule: *A customer service request must be brought to the attention of a supervisor if the request is not resolved within 4 hours.*

In this example we find: (1) the action item *customer service request*, (2) the party *supervisor*, (3) the escalation criteria *if not resolved*, and (4) the timing criteria *within 4 hours*.

Best Practices

Definitional rules address knowledge; what *people* do is another matter. Having flesh-and-blood people involved 'in the loop' makes a big difference. Best practices in designing **business processes** with business rules *and people* include:

1. **Avoid mixing definitional and behavioral criteria in the same business rule.** Do people 'in the loop' need to abide by specific results from evaluating definitional rules? If so, specify some behavioral rule(s). For example, derivation rules may determine whether or not an applicant for insurance satisfies all prerequisites. Some separate behavioral rule(s) can indicate whether the decision-maker(s) in the loop *must* accept a qualified applicant — or must *not* accept an *unqualified* applicant.

> Behavioral rules should indicate whether people must abide by results from evaluating definitional rules.

2. **Separate decision tasks from tasks for people to take business action.** Knowledge-rich tasks (e.g., determining the suitability of an applicant) can be based on definitional rules; the take-action tasks (e.g., hiring the applicant) can be guided by behavioral rules.

> Tasks for making operational decisions should be separated from tasks involving business action.

3. **Consider the cost of business rules in developing the business process.** In business terms, it would be *very* costly (if even possible) to gather *all* the data that *any* definitional rule potentially applied in a business process might need. For example, a car insurance company might have the business rule: *An applicant for car insurance is never considered qualified if the applicant is less than the minimum driving age.* Other business rules might involve creditworthiness (which could involve an extensive credit check), previous driving history (which could require requesting records from the state), and so on. If it can

be determined right from the start the applicant isn't old enough, that's obviously something you want to do. So a basic goal in designing business processes with business rules and people is *work avoidance* (no pun intended). Always test the cheapest rules first wherever possible.

> Avoid unnecessary work in a business process
> by testing cheap rules first.

Summary

A **business process** model is an end-to-end, results-oriented view of the business tasks appropriate for a planned, optimal response to a significant **business event**. **Business rules** capture the logic needed to guide and support such activity, but do not substitute for the business process itself.

Business process models can be greatly simplified by taking the business rules out and addressing them separately. A result is stable business processes that serve as a framework for managing cross-organizational business activity.

A business process model cannot possibly address hundreds or thousands of business rules directly. What to do? Do what comes naturally — maintain a separate **rulebook**, as in football. The rulebook becomes a vital new resource for managing rapid change in business practices.

> Do what comes naturally — maintain a separate rulebook.

Chapter 12

Envisioning Really Smart Systems: Dynamic, Thin, Throwaway Procedures

In the National Football League (NFL), if a play is not working for a team, it will be gone from its playbook in short order (possibly along with a coach or two). New plays can be deployed rapidly. In effect, the plays are essentially *throwaways* — cheap enough to discard readily, with minimum disruption or cost. Businesses urgently need something similar — throwaway **procedures** cheap enough to replace readily when they no longer work well (make 'yardage') for the business.

The reason NFL plays can be treated as throwaways is that the **know-how** to run them is embodied elsewhere — in the scoreboard, in the skills of the players, in the heads of the coaches, and most importantly, in the NFL rulebook.

An automated system that supports throwaway procedures is a *smart* system. **Business rules** play a major role. **Smart systems** take us to a whole new threshold of agility.

> Smart systems based on business rules take us
> to a whole new threshold of agility.

Before we begin, let me clarify something. All definitional rules are automatable; a system that removes evaluation of definitional rules as an application concern (i.e., one that provides a facility for automated **decisions**) is already a smart one. That's huge, but it's just a start. A *really* **smart system** is one that also automatically handles **flash points**, especially for behavioral rules. Read on!

Computational Models for Really Smart Systems

Note to the Reader
At this point, I need to discuss how business-rule-friendly **procedures** should be designed. If your interest is primarily business rules, you won't miss too much by skipping this section and continuing with the section "Behavioral Rules in Really Smart Systems" on page 134. Be sure not to miss that one though!

In designing a system, you create a computational model (sometimes called a system model). John Zachman notes that a computational model involves

"... surrogates for ... real-world things so that the real-world things can be managed on a scale and at a distance that is not possible in the real world." So, to design **smart systems** you first need to identify the necessary **surrogates**.

For business rules, the surrogates for real-world business things and how they relate are **facts**. A **concept model** (**structured business vocabulary**) enables you to organize facts massively based on real business vocabulary (**terms** and **wordings**). For example for the **verb concept** worded *customer places order*, we might have the fact *Global Supply, Inc. has placed the order A601288*. The reason *concept model* is preferred over *fact model*, incidentally, is simply that facts are surrogates, not the real-world things.

> Facts are surrogates for real-world business things and how they relate.

Facts serve to define **state** in smart systems. That's the **semantic** way to define state; any other scheme (e.g., process **tokens**) is <u>un</u>semantic. Facts, however, basically just sit there until something happens. Something has to happen to stir them up (change state) — you need **events** for that. Events can occur:

- Based on execution of some orderly process designed to do things in a certain way.
- More or less spontaneously (ad hoc), independently of any modeled process.

Either way (and both are valid), many events that occur are bound to be flash points for business rules. That's where things get really interesting. But let's hold that thought until we develop more groundwork.

What do we mean by *event* in smart systems? We simply mean any change in state — that is, any change in the facts. What kinds of event can happen for a fact? What can you do with one? An order clerk might:

- Request it. For example: *Obtain the credit rating for a customer.*
- Store it. For example: *Store an order placed by a customer.*
- Display it. For example: *Display customer's current account balance.*
- Communicate it. For example: *Insert a special order into a supervisor's work queue for approval.*

Support for the order clerk's system activity would require other kinds of surrogates as well, for example:

- *Work queues.* The supervisor's work queue is actually a *surrogate* for a face-to-face interaction between a supervisor and an order clerk each time a special order is received.
- *Graphical user interfaces (GUIs).* The supervisor's GUI for displaying orders in the queue is actually a *surrogate* for the flesh-and-blood order clerk.

A good name for an orderly process in a computational model is *procedure*. A **procedure** [MWUD] is simply: *1a: a particular way of doing or of going about the accomplishment of something ... b(3): a series of steps followed in a regular orderly definite way.* The key phrase is *series of steps*.

A procedure is simply a series of steps for manipulating surrogates standing in for real-world things. One thing you won't see in a *smart* procedure is business rules. Now you might see flash points, but that's a different matter. Under **Rule Independence**, business rules are externalized from procedures into a rulebook. That's how you get *thin* processes.

> You get thin processes by
> externalizing business rules into a rulebook.

A small digression here. If you examine traditional application code closely, you find that only a relatively small portion is actually devoted to the real steps of a procedure. Much of the code is devoted to edits, validations, derivations, and calculations — in other words, to business rules. That's not the end of it. The code also has to detect **violations** of the

behavioral rules in the first place, then map out appropriate responses. So by taking the business rules out, we're talking about *really* thin procedures.

In a **smart system**, procedures relate to business rules via flash points. Flash points are the key to the puzzle. They are how you can create highly *dynamic* procedures — ones that flow dutifully along a series of steps yet that, to an observer, would probably seem *indeterminate*. We still need more groundwork, but you'll see when we get to behavioral rules.

> Highly *dynamic* procedures — ones that seem *indeterminate* — result from managing flash points for business rules separately.

Collaboration in Really Smart Systems

A football play is a good analogy for a procedure. A diagram of a football play is literally represented as a collection of orchestrated steps needed to

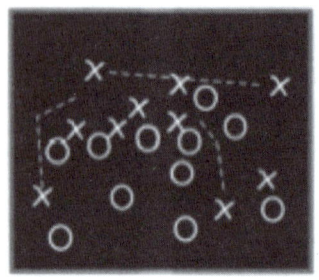

accomplish the desired result (advance the ball). It's nothing more and nothing less. No business rules — or penalties for violating them — are embedded within it. A play simply focuses on what needs to be done.

A **procedure** provides a recipe or pattern, a series of steps, for manipulating **surrogates**. A procedure might be used to take a customer order, evaluate a medical claim, book a reservation, assign a teacher to a class, and so on. Often a procedure is undertaken in response to something that somebody does (e.g., a customer placing an order). A procedure can also be undertaken in response to some timing criteria (e.g., when to bill customers), or to some predefined condition (e.g., inventory quantity on hand is below a certain threshold). In both these latter cases, appropriate criteria for automatically initiating the procedures can be expressed as business rules.

> A procedure provides a recipe or pattern
> for manipulating surrogates.

Series of steps is an apt description of a **procedure**; *prescribed* series of *requests* is even better.

- By *request* I mean request for action by some surrogate — one of the same kinds of surrogate and action mentioned earlier. Such requests are often (but not always) handled by software components or services presumed to execute. Such software components might include some DBMS or factbase management system (the equivalent of a DBMS except for facts), GUIs, service providers (e.g., print routines), interfaces to legacy systems, work queues, special-purpose business rule analyzers, constraint solvers, and so on.

- By *prescribed* I mean that the series of steps *can* be followed to achieve the desired results, *not* that they must be. For example, there might be one or more other series of steps (procedures) you can follow to achieve the same results. Or if you really know your stuff (think great chefs of Paris), you might achieve the results more or less ad hoc (sparking 'spontaneous' events seemingly out of the blue). To say *must be followed* would represent a business rule about sequencing. It's better to handle such matters by expressing business rules placing restrictions on **states** (e.g., required antecedents).

People in Really Smart Systems

In many respects, the most important originators or recipients of requests in procedures are people. People, after all, still do a lot of actual work! These people might be either *inside* the company (that is, workers) or *outside* the company (e.g., customers).

Although these people might be seen as 'users', we like **actor** better. Here's why. The term *user* suggests outside beneficiaries of system services, whose own work and interactions are outside scope. *Actor*, in contrast, suggests someone whose own activity or **role** is integral to understanding and doing the work. An actor is someone whose own work is definitely *within* scope.

We do have to be careful here. We're not talking about putting *actual* actors into procedures — that is, real live flesh-and-blood people. You can't put real people into an automated system! Instead, we're actually talking about surrogates that stand in for the actors. Generally these surrogates would be specified as roles (the people kind), but for specific people, they could also be communication links (e.g., an email address).

> A procedure involves people too.

What can human actors do to move work along in procedures? Two things: (a) perform actions — manually or otherwise — and (b) make requests for action to software components or to other actors.

Here then is the emerging vision for orchestrating work in **smart systems** — many kinds of actors, some human and some software, collaborating according to really thin, throwaway procedures. By the way, because of the prominent place of human actors in all this, we call (smart) procedures **scripts**. After all, a procedure essentially *scripts* work for a collection of actors. For this discussion, however, I'll stick to *procedure*.

> A procedure prescribes a scripted collaboration
> involving both people and software.

Behavioral Rules in Really Smart Systems

Now we get to the good stuff. Here's what you need to do to prepare business rules for their role in **smart systems**.

1. *What **enforcement level** you want for each behavioral rule.* Possible enforcement levels for **behavioral rules** and their implications for designing procedures are given in Table 12–1. The default enforcement level, incidentally, is *strictly enforced*.

2. *How (if at all) you want to respond to a **breach** of each business rule.* Appropriate **breach responses** can be given by: (a) some other business rule(s), (b) some procedure(s), or (c) both. (The most important breach responses are generally for behavioral rules — remember only behavioral rules can actually be violated — so from here on I'll say **violation** rather than *breach*.) These other business rule(s) generally prescribe appropriate sanction(s); the procedures(s) generally layout appropriate response(s).

> Plan responses to breaches of a business rule
> as additional business rules or procedures.

Table 12–1. Enforcement Levels for Behavioral Rules and Their Implications for Designing Procedures.

Enforcement Level	Description	Implication for Designing Procedures
strictly enforced	If an actor violates the behavioral rule, the actor cannot escape sanction(s).	When a violation is detected, the event producing the violation is automatically prevented, if possible, and a designated violation response, if any, is invoked automatically.
deferred enforcement	The behavioral rule is strictly enforced, but such enforcement may be delayed — e.g., until another actor with required skills and proper authorization can become involved.	When a violation is detected, the event producing the violation is allowed, and the relevant work is handed off to another worker (possibly by insertion into a work queue). Additional business rules giving timing criteria may be desirable to ensure that action is taken within an appropriate timeframe.
override by pre-authorized actor	The behavioral rule is enforced, but an actor with proper before-the-fact authorization may override it.	When a violation is detected, if the actor involved is pre-authorized, that actor is given an opportunity to override the rule. Overrides by actor and business rule should be tracked for subsequent review.
override with real-time waiver	The behavioral rule is enforced, but an actor may request a real-time waiver from another actor having before-the-fact authorization to give such waivers.	When a violation is detected, the actor involved is given an opportunity to interactively request a waiver from a duly-authorized actor. Additional business rules giving timing criteria may be desirable to ensure that some action is taken within an appropriate timeframe. Waivers should be tracked by actor and business rule for subsequent review.
post-justified override	The behavioral rule may be overridden by an actor who is not explicitly authorized; however, if the override is subsequently deemed inappropriate, the actor may be subject to sanction(s).	When an override of a violation occurs, a review item (with all relevant details) should be inserted into the work queue of an appropriate actor for review and possible action.
override with explanation	The behavioral rule may be overridden simply by providing an explanation.	When a violation is detected, the actor involved is given an opportunity to override the business rule by providing a mandatory explanation. Overrides should be tracked by actor and business rule for subsequent review.
guideline	Suggested, but not enforced.	When a violation is detected, the actor involved (if authorized) is simply informed/reminded of the behavioral rule.

About Sleepers

Not included in Table 12–1 is 'not evaluated'. But that's not an **enforcement level**; it could also apply to definitional rules. I call a business rule indicated not to be evaluated a **sleeper**. A sleeper might literally be just for show (public consumption); more likely, it is not being evaluated because it is pending or retired; deemed inapplicable or overly expensive; etc.

If a behavioral rule is not automatable, you also need to determine how to detect violations. To illustrate, let's work through an example — the offside rule in the game of football: *A player must not be offside.* (Some definitional rule(s) would be needed for *offside*, but let's ignore that here.)

1. *What enforcement level do you want for the offside rule?* Let's say *strictly enforced.*

2. *How (if at all) do you want to react to a violation of the offside rule?* You need another business rule prescribing the appropriate sanction: *The offside team in a play must be penalized five yards or half the distance to the team's own goal line, whichever is less.* We also have a special procedure: *Pace off yardage penalized.*

3. *How will you detect violations of the offside rule?* Since the offside rule is not automatable (as far as we know), detection is assigned to the line judge as a job responsibility. *The line judge watches the play, blows a whistle, throws a flag, stops the play, etc.*

Automatic Flash Points

If the behavioral rule *is* automatable (and a very great many are), that's wonderful news. In a really smart system, you can assume there is an execution-time software platform or service that knows about all **flash points** and can detect them automatically. Call it the **flash-point service**. Nothing at all needs to be scripted in procedures for detection of violations! The hidden hand of the flash-point service makes procedures *intrinsically* smart.

A really smart system relies on a flash-point service to automatically detect violations of behavioral rules.

To illustrate an automatable **smart procedure** let's first walk through a really dumb **scenario**:

- We have the behavioral rule: *An order must have a ship-to address.*
- We decide we want the business rule to be *strictly enforced.*
- We do not specify any special response or recourse for a violation.

Now we watch what happens when the (barely) smart procedure executes:

1. A worker initiates the procedure: *Take customer order.*

2. The worker's activity produces an **event**: *An order is created.*

3. The flash-point service checks whether the event is a flash point. The flash-point service determines that the event is a flash point for the behavioral rule: *An order must have a ship-to address.*

4. The flash-point service checks whether the worker has actually given a ship-to address with the order.

5. Suppose the worker has not done so. The flash-point service causes the event to be rejected — that is, the action (request) fails and the order is not created.

At their strictest, behavioral rules are very narrow-minded. Either the actor plays by the rules, or the work is not accepted. If any question about the quality of the work arises — that is, about its correctness or consistency — the work is simply rejected. In other words, straight-laced behavioral rules *insist* upon the highest quality and do so by active, real-time intervention in ongoing work. Such **real-time compliance** for behavioral rules is a distinctive feature of really smart systems.

> **Real-time compliance is inherent in really smart systems.**

That execution was almost laughably unfriendly. I call a behavioral rule set up to be strictly enforced without any recourse a **meany**. Generally, that's not going to be a best practice — *unless* the violation represents attempted fraud, theft, or attack. Then 'meanness' (and appropriate countermeasures) is exactly the right response(!).

But let's suppose the violation is an innocent one. If the worker is authorized and capable, the flash-point service should at the very least present a **guidance message** (minimally the business rule statement) to the worker. It thereby informs (enlightens) the worker about the business practice, so the worker can correct the problem (by giving a *ship-to-address*) and avoid it in the future.

Can a smart procedure be even friendlier? *Of course!* That brings us to re-use.

Flash-Point Re-Use

For smart procedures you want much more than simple re-use through everyday modular design. (Refer to the sidebar.) Re-use of software is good; re-use of procedures based on behavioral rules is *really smart*.

Everyday Modular Design in Procedures

Re-use based on modular design occurs when one **procedure** simply uses (requests) some other procedure to do a step of its own work. Since the second procedure is not embedded within the first, the second can be requested (re-used) by *other* procedures as well. For example, the procedure *Fill out address* could be potentially (re)used by the procedures: *Take customer order, Record prospect information, Create shipment, Hire employee,* and so on. This kind of reuse is desirable, but involves no special use of business rules.

Specifically, you want *flash-point re-use* of procedures. The mechanics of flash-point re-use work like this:

1. A procedure for undertaking work in normal circumstances is invoked as the designated response to the **breach** of a business rule.

2. That procedure kicks off automatically whenever a breach of the business rule is detected.

3. If the actor elects to follow through with this second procedure, it steps the actor through correction of the problem. Once resolved, the actor can move on with the original work as scripted by the first procedure.

> Really smart systems support flash-point re-use
> of procedures based on business rules.

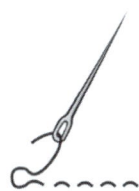

The net result of flash-point re-use is a truly *dynamic* work environment, one where procedures are stitched together automatically just-in-time based on what any given actor knows (or doesn't) about current business practices. To an outside observer, the resulting work environment would probably *seem* indeterminate. But that's just the grand illusion of really smart systems.

Table 12–2 illustrates flash-point re-use, step-by-step, for this simple **scenario**:

Procedure: *Take customer order.*
This procedure is performed by an order entry clerk.

Behavioral Rule: *A customer who places an order over $1,000 must hold an account.*

Violation Response: Invoke the procedure *Establish customer account.* Let's say this is the procedure normally used to set up accounts, so there's a good chance it would be already familiar to the order entry clerk.

> A work environment that seems indeterminate
> is the grand illusion of really smart systems.

Specifying Violation Responses

A **flash-point service** for really **smart systems** would support context-sensitive **violation responses** for each **behavioral rule**, as needed. For example, the violation response given in the illustration for the behavioral rule might be selectively specified for:

- A particular **procedure**.
- A particular **flash point**.
- A particular flash point in a particular procedure.
- A given class of **actor**.
- An individual actor.
- etc.

Table 12–2. Scenario for Flash-Point Re-Use of a Procedure.

	Step-by-Step Activity	Simple Scenario
1.	A worker performs a procedure.	A worker (order entry clerk) performs a procedure (*Take customer order*) to take an order.
2.	The worker makes a request under that procedure.	The worker (order entry clerk) makes a request (that an order be created).
3.	The request produces a change in state.	Change in state (creation of facts about the order) is attempted.
4.	The event results in the flash-point evaluation of relevant business rules, if any.	This event causes the behavioral rule to be evaluated: *A customer who places an order over $1000 must hold an account.*
5.	A breach of one of these business rules, let's suppose, is detected.	Let's say the customer holds no account, so a violation of the behavioral rule above is detected.
6.	Another procedure (designated beforehand) is invoked automatically.	*Establish customer account* had been designated beforehand as the procedure to be invoked for a violation of this behavioral rule.
7.	This other procedure offers the capability needed for the original worker (or possibly someone else) to correct the error that caused the breach.	The order entry clerk is offered the opportunity to perform the procedure *Establish customer account.*
8.	Supposing such work is undertaken under the offered procedure (not a given) ...	The order entry clerk elects to perform the procedure.
9.	And supposing such work is deemed satisfactory with respect to the business rule ...	This work successfully corrects the original violation of the behavioral rule — the customer now holds an account.
10.	Then work can continue under the *original* procedure from where it left off.	The order entry clerk resumes work under the original procedure, *Take customer order*, from the point it was interrupted. For example, the next action might be to schedule the order's fulfillment.

Summary

Let's take one last, hard look at *agility*. Generally, the more *granular* the specifications for a system, the more *adaptable* it will be. Specifications in **smart systems** organized around **business rules** are *highly* granular in these ways:

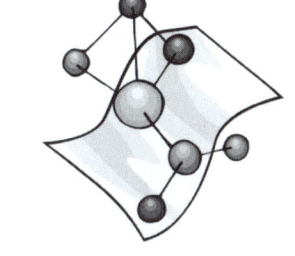

- Each business rule is specified independently of processes.

- Each business rule is generally specified independently of **events**.

- Each **breach response** for a business rule is generally specified independently of **procedures**.

- The **enforcement level** for a **behavioral rule** is specified independently of the rule itself, and generally independently of events and procedures.

In really smart systems, the **flash-point service** for business rules is the hidden hand for dynamic, thin, throwaway procedures.

> Specifications in really smart systems are highly granular, yielding true software agility.

Business Rules Manifesto
The Principles of Rule Independence
by Business Rules Group[1]

Article 1. Primary Requirements, Not Secondary
1.1. Rules are a first-class citizen of the requirements world.
1.2. Rules are essential for, and a discrete part of, business models and technology models.

Article 2. Separate From Processes, Not Contained In Them
2.1. Rules are explicit constraints on behavior and/or provide support to behavior.
2.2. Rules are not process and not procedure. They should not be contained in either of these.
2.3. Rules apply *across* processes and procedures. There should be one cohesive body of rules, enforced consistently across all relevant areas of business activity.

Article 3. Deliberate Knowledge, Not A By-Product
3.1. Rules build on facts, and facts build on concepts as expressed by terms.
3.2. Terms express business concepts; facts make assertions about these concepts; rules constrain and support these facts.
3.3. Rules must be explicit. No rule is ever assumed about any concept or fact.
3.4. Rules are basic to what the business knows about itself — that is, to basic business knowledge.
3.5. Rules need to be nurtured, protected, and managed.

Article 4. Declarative, Not Procedural
4.1. Rules should be expressed declaratively in natural-language sentences for the business audience.
4.2. If something cannot be expressed, then it is not a rule.
4.3. A set of statements is declarative only if the set has no implicit sequencing.
4.4. Any statements of rules that require constructs other than terms and facts imply assumptions about a system implementation.
4.5. A rule is distinct from any enforcement defined for it. A rule and its enforcement are separate concerns.
4.6. Rules should be defined independently of responsibility for the *who*, *where*, *when*, or *how* of their enforcement.
4.7. Exceptions to rules are expressed by other rules.

Article 5. Well-Formed Expression, Not Ad Hoc
5.1. Business rules should be expressed in such a way that they can be validated for correctness by business people.
5.2. Business rules should be expressed in such a way that they can be verified against each other for consistency.

5.3.   Formal logics, such as predicate logic, are fundamental to well-formed expression of rules in business terms, as well as to the technologies that implement business rules.

Article 6. Rule-Based Architecture, Not Indirect Implementation

6.1.   A business rules application is intentionally built to accommodate continuous change in business rules. The platform on which the application runs should support such continuous change.

6.2.   Executing rules directly — for example in a rules engine — is a better implementation strategy than transcribing the rules into some procedural form.

6.3.   A business rule system must always be able to explain the reasoning by which it arrives at conclusions or takes action.

6.4.   Rules are based on truth values. How a rule's truth value is determined or maintained is hidden from users.

6.5.   The relationship between events and rules is generally many-to-many.

Article 7. Rule-Guided Processes, Not Exception-Based Programming

7.1.   Rules define the boundary between acceptable and unacceptable business activity.

7.2.   Rules often require special or selective handling of detected violations. Such rule violation activity is activity like any other activity.

7.3.   To ensure maximum consistency and reusability, the handling of unacceptable business activity should be separable from the handling of acceptable business activity.

Article 8. For the Sake of the Business, Not Technology

8.1.   Rules are about business practice and guidance; therefore, rules are motivated by business goals and objectives and are shaped by various influences.

8.2.   Rules always cost the business something.

8.3.   The cost of rule enforcement must be balanced against business risks, and against business opportunities that might otherwise be lost.

8.4.   'More rules' is not better. Usually fewer 'good rules' is better.

8.5.   An effective system can be based on a small number of rules. Additional, more discriminating rules can be subsequently added, so that over time the system becomes smarter.

Article 9. Of, By, and For Business People, Not IT People

9.1.   Rules should arise from knowledgeable business people.

9.2.   Business people should have tools available to help them formulate, validate, and manage rules.

9.3.   Business people should have tools available to help them verify business rules against each other for consistency.

Article 10. Managing Business Logic, Not Hardware/Software Platforms

10.1. Business rules are a vital business asset.

10.2. In the long run, rules are more important to the business than hardware / software platforms.

10.3. Business rules should be organized and stored in such a way that they can be readily redeployed to new hardware/software platforms.

10.4. Rules, and the ability to change them effectively, are fundamental to improving business adaptability.

Glossary

Reference Sources	
[MWUD]	*Merriam-Webster Unabridged Dictionary* (Version 2.5). [2000]. Merriam-Webster Inc.
[SBVR]	*Semantics of Business Vocabulary and Business Rules (SBVR).* [January 2008]. Object Management Group.

actor [business process]: *any participant in a* **business process**

actor [smart procedure]: *any participant in a* **smart procedure** *as represented by its* **surrogate**

advice: [SBVR] *an* **element of guidance** *that something is permissible or possible, that there is no* **rule** *against it*

anomaly: [MWUD] 3: *something irregular or abnormal*

behavioral rule: [SBVR] *a* **business rule** *that there is an obligation concerning conduct, action, practice, or* **procedure***; a* **business rule** *whose purpose is to shape (govern) day-to-day business activity and prevent undesirable situations* **(states)** *that could occur at any of various points in time*

binary verb concept: *a* **verb concept** *that involves exactly two* **noun concepts**

breach (of a business rule): *a failure to satisfy a* **business rule** *at one of its* **flash points**

breach response: *the appropriate response specified for a* **breach** *of a* **business rule**

business event: *an* **event** *requiring the business to respond, usually in a non-trivial way and often following some pattern of activity developed in advance, for example, a* **business process** *model*

business governance: *a process, organizational function, set of techniques, and systematic approach for creating and deploying* **policies** *and* **business rules** *into day-to-day business operations*

business policy: *an* **element of guidance** *given for* **business governance** *that is not* **practicable**

business process: *the tasks required for an enterprise to satisfy a planned response to a* **business event** *from beginning to end with a focus on the* **roles** *of* **actors***, rather than the* **actors***' day-to-day job*

business rule: [SBVR] *a* **rule** *that is* **under business jurisdiction**

business vocabulary: *see* **structured business vocabulary**

case: *a particular situation;* [MWUD] 1b: *a set of circumstances constituting a problem: a matter for consideration or decision: as (1): a circumstance or situation*

categorization: *a special element of structure in which one class of things is a* **category** *of some other class of things*

categorization scheme: *a scheme used to categorize things into two or more* **categories** *(e.g., 'gender' is the scheme for categorizing people as 'male' and 'female')*

category: *a class of things whose meaning is more restrictive, but otherwise compliant with, some other class of things (e.g., person and organization are* **categories** *of party)*

classification: *a special element of structure in which a thing is an* **instance** *of a class of things*

composition: *see* **whole-part structure**

concept: [MWUD] *something conceived in the mind : THOUGHT, IDEA, NOTION*

concept model: *the* **semantic** *blueprint of a* **structured business vocabulary**

ConceptSpeak™: *the Business Rule Solutions, LLC (BRS) set of conventions, guidelines, and techniques for defining* **terms***, designing a* **concept model***, and developing a* **structured business vocabulary**

conflict: [MWUD] 1a: *clash, competition, or mutual interference of opposing or incompatible forces or qualities*

conflict (business rules): *an* **anomaly** *within or among some* **business rule(s)** *such that multiple* **states** *or* **outcomes** *are required that cannot all be satisfied simultaneously*

consideration: *a factor in making an* **operational business decision***; something that can be resolved into two or more* **cases**

corporate memory: *the ability to recall* **governance decisions** *made in the past, understand their motivation, and trace their impacts*

CRUD: *create, retrieve, update, or delete*

decision: *a determination requiring* **know-how***; the resolving of a question by reasoning*

decision table: *a structured means of visualizing* **business rules** *in rows and columns*

declarative (statement): [MWUD] 2: *constituting a statement that can be either true or false*

definition: [MWUD] 2: *a word or phrase expressing the essential nature of a person or thing or class of persons or of things : an answer to the question "what is x?" or "what is an x?"*

definitional rule: [SBVR] *a* **rule** *that is intended as a definitional criterion*

element of guidance: *a* **business policy**, **business rule**, *or an* **advice**

elementary verb concept: *a* **verb concept** *that cannot be broken down into two or more other* **verb concepts**, *each with fewer* **noun concepts**, *without losing knowledge*

enforcement level: *how strictly a* **behavioral rule** *is to be enforced*

error message: *see* **guidance message**

event: [MWUD] 1a(1): *something that happens*

exception: [MWUD] 2: *one that is excepted or taken out from others *almost every general rule has its exceptions**

exception (business rule): *a* **business rule** *that addresses some set of circumstances viewed as an* **exception** *or exceptional* **case** *in day-to-day business activity*

fact: [MWUD] 5 : *an assertion, statement, or information containing or purporting to contain something having objective reality*

flash point: *an* **event** *when a* **business rule** *needs to be evaluated*

flash-point service: *an execution-time software platform or service that knows about all* **flash points** *and can detect them automatically*

GBRS: *see* **general rulebook system**

general rulebook system (GBRS): *an automated, specialized, business-level platform for managing* **business rules** *and* **business vocabulary**

governance: *see* **business governance**

governance process: *a series of actions and checkpoints (i.e., a workflow) indicating who should be doing what, and when, with respect to deploying* **policies** *and* **business rules**

governing rule: *any law, act, statute, legal determination, regulation, contract, agreement, deal, service level agreement, certification, warranty, license,* **business policy***, etc., from which* **business rules** *can be interpreted*

guidance message: *a message provided at a* **flash point** *for a* **business rule**

guideline: *a* **behavioral rule** *that is active but not enforced*

incremental design: *developing a system through repeated cycles (iteratively) and in smaller portions at a time (incrementally)*

instance: *something in the real world*

IPSpeak™: *the Business Rule Solutions, LLC (BRS) methodology for capturing, expressing, analyzing, and managing the operational-level intellectual property (IP) of the business — specifically,* **business rules***, decision logic,* **structured business vocabulary (concept models)***, and strategy*

know-how: [MWUD] *... accumulated practical skill or expertness ... especially: technical knowledge, ability, skill, or expertness of this sort*

meany: *a* **behavioral rule** *whose* **enforcement level** *indicates strict rejection of* **violations** *without recourse*

modal: [MWUD "mode"] *... having to do with the manner in which a logical proposition (e.g., a* **business rule***) is asserted*

n-ary verb concept: *a* **verb concept** *that involves more than two* **noun concepts**

nominalization: [MWUD] *the process or result of forming a noun or noun phrase from a clause or a verb*

noun concept: *the* **concept** *that a* **term** *represents*

objectification: *the* **noun concept** *that results from* **objectifying** *a* **verb concept**

objectify: *to cause a* **verb concept** *to become or to assume the character of a* **noun concept** *(e.g., the* **verb concept** *'student enrolls in course offering' could be* **objectified** *as 'enrollment')*

operational business decision: *a* **decision** *arising in day-to-day business activity*

operative rule: [SBVR] *see* **behavioral rule**

outcome: *a result or conclusion that is deemed appropriate for some* **case**

participle: [MWUD]: *a word having the characteristics of both verb and adjective*

partitive structure: *see* **whole-part structure**

past participle: [MWUD]: *a* **participle** *that typically expresses completed action … as arrived* in: *the ship, arrived at last, signals for a tug.*

point of knowledge: *where operational business* **know-how** *is produced or consumed — i.e., where* **business rules** *are developed, applied, assessed, re-used, and ultimately retired*

POK: *see* **point of knowledge**

policy: *see* **business policy**

practicable: [MWUD] 1: *possible to practice or perform : capable of being put into practice, done, or accomplished* [MWUD 2a]: *capable of being used : USABLE*

practicable [element of guidance]: [SBVR]: *an* **element of guidance** *that is ready to deploy into business operations such that it can satisfy the following test: an* **element of guidance** *sufficiently detailed and precise that a person who knows the* **element of guidance** *can apply it effectively and consistently in relevant circumstances to know what behavior is acceptable or not, or how something is understood*

procedural (statement): *a statement included in a series of other statements to specify a* **procedure**

procedure: [MWUD] 1b(3): *a series of steps followed in a regular orderly definite way*

prohibited antecedent: *a* **state** *that if achieved by an* **instance** *precludes some other* **state** *being achieved by that same* **instance**

property: [MWUD] 1a: *a quality or trait belonging to a person or thing*

real-time compliance: *enforcement of* **business rules** *at their* **flash points**

role (business): [MWUD] 1b1: *a part played by a business* **actor**; [MWUD] 2: *a function performed by someone or something in a particular situation, process, or operation*

role (verb concept): *a* **noun concept** *that reflects how another* **noun concept** *is viewed in the context of a* **verb concept**

rule: [MWUD] 1a: *guide for conduct or action* 1f: *one of a set of usually official regulations by which an activity (as a sport) is governed [e.g.,] *the infield fly rule* *the rules of professional basketball** [MWUD 'criteria'] 2: *a standard on which a decision or judgment may be based*

Rule Independence: *the externalization, unification, and management of* **rules** *separately from processes*

rulebook: *the collection of* **elements of guidance** *for a business, along with the statements,* **terms**, **definitions**, *and* **wordings** *that support them*

rulebook management: *the skills, techniques, and processes needed to express, analyze, trace, retain, and manage the* **business rules** *used for day-to-day business operations*

RuleSpeak®: *the Business Rule Solutions (BRS) set of guidelines and conventions for expressing* **business rules** *in a concise, business-friendly fashion using structured natural language*

SBVR: *see* **Semantics of Business Vocabularies and Business Rules**

scenario: [MWUD]: *a sequence of* **events** *especially when imagined*

script: *see* **smart procedure**

semantic(s): [MWUD (noun) – semantics]: *a system or theory of meaning* [MWUD (adjective) – semantic]: *of or relating to meaning in language*

Semantics of Business Vocabularies and Business Rules (SBVR): *the standard initially published in January 2008 by the Object Management Group (OMG), whose central goal is to enable the full* **semantics** *of* **business rules** *and other forms of business communication to be captured, encoded, analyzed (for* **anomalies***), and transferred between machines (thereby achieving* **semantic** *interoperability)*

simple consideration: *a* **consideration** *with two or three* **cases**

single-sourcing: *specifying* **business rules** *only once no matter how many places deployed*

sleeper: *a* **business rule** *not to be evaluated (i.e., inactive)*

smart architecture: *the architecture for a* **smart system**

smart procedure: *a thin, throwaway* **procedure** *in a* **smart system**

smart system: *a system that removes evaluation of* **definitional rules** *as an application concern (i.e., one that provides a facility for automated* **decisions***) and that automatically handles* **flash points***, especially for* **behavioral rules**

state: [MWUD] 1a: *a mode or condition of being;*
[MWUD – mode 6]: *a condition or state of being : a manifestation, form, or manner of arrangement*

structural rule: [SBVR] *see* **definitional rule**

structured business vocabulary: *the set of* **terms** *and their* **definitions**, *and all* **wordings**, *that organize operational business* **know-how**

subsumption: *an* **anomaly** *among* **business rule(s)** *that all require or disallow the same* **state**, *except that one* **business rule** *requires or disallows the* **state** *for a superset of* **cases** *than the other* **business rule**

surrogate: [MWUD] 2a: *something that replaces or serves as a substitute for another*

term: [MWUD] 8a: *a word or expression that has a precisely-limited meaning in some uses or is peculiar to a science, art, profession, trade, or special subject*

token (process): *a pointer for a thread in a process or computer program serving to indicate current position*

unary verb concept: *a* **verb concept** *that involves exactly one* **noun concept**

under business jurisdiction: [SBVR] *a* **rule** *that the business can opt to change or discard*

validation: *ensuring the correctness of some* **business rule(s)** *with respect to business purpose*

verb concept: *something specific that can be known about one or more* **noun concept(s)** *important to business operations (e.g., that a customer can place an order)*

verb concept wording: [SBVR] *see* **wording**

verbalization model: *see* **structured business vocabulary**

verification: *assessing the fitness of some* **business rule(s)** *with respect to logical consistency; looking for* **anomalies** *in (some)* **business rule(s)** *(usually two or more in combination)*

violation (of a behavioral rule): *a* **breach** *of a* **behavioral rule**

violation message: *see* **guidance message**

violation response: *see* **breach response**

vocabulary: *see* **structured business vocabulary**

whole-part structure: *a special collection of one or more* **binary verb concepts** *that together describe how a thing of one class of things (the whole) is composed of things of (typically) two or more other classes of things (the parts)*

wording: *an expression including one or more* **terms** *and a verb or verb phrase organized appropriately to represent a* **verb concept** *(e.g.,* 'customer places order')

References

Berry, Daniel M., Erik Kamsties, Michael M. Krieger, and Willenken
Loh Stris Lee & Tran. [November 2003]. *From Contract Drafting
to Software Specification: Linguistic Sources of Ambiguity:
A Handbook*, (Version 1.0). ["Ambiguity Handbook"].
Available at: http://se.uwaterloo.ca/~dberry/

Burlton, Roger T. [2001]. *Business Process Management: Profiting
from Success*. Indianapolis, IN: Sams Publishing.

Business Rules Group. [September 2007]. *The Business Motivation
Model ~ Business Governance in a Volatile World*, (Ver. 1.3).
Available at: http://www.BusinessRulesGroup.org
Note: An adopted standard of the Object Management Group (OMG).

Business Rules Group. [2003]. *Business Rules Manifesto ~ The
Principles of Rule Independence*, (Ver. 1.2).
Available at: http://www.BusinessRulesGroup.org
Note: In English as well as more than a dozen other languages.

Business Rules Group. [July 2000]. *Defining Business Rules ~
What Are They Really?* (4th ed).
Available at: http://www.BusinessRulesGroup.org
Note: Formerly known as the *GUIDE Business Rules Project Report*, (1995).

Crystal, David. [2005]. *How Languages Work*. Woodstock, NY: The
Overlook Press, Peter Mayer Publishers, Inc.

Editors of BRCommunity.com. [November 2008]. "A Brief History of
the Business Rule Approach," *Business Rules Journal*, Vol. 9, No. 11.
Available at: http://www.BRCommunity.com/a2008/b448.html

Halpin, Terry (with Tony Morgan). [2008]. *Information Modeling and
Relational Databases*, (2nd Ed.), San Francisco, CA: Morgan Kaufmann.

ISO 1087-1. [2000]. *Terminology Work — Vocabulary, Part 1: Theory
and Application*.

ISO 704. [2000]. *Terminology Work — Principles and Methods*.

Lam, Gladys S. W. [May/June 1998]. "Business Knowledge — Packaged
in a Policy Charter," *DataToKnowledge Newsletter*, Vol. 26, No. 3.
Available at: http://www.BRCommunity.com/a1998/a385.html

Merriam-Webster Unabridged Dictionary, (Version 2.5). [2000].
Merriam-Webster Inc.

Nijssen, Sjir. [July 1981]. *An Architecture for Knowledge Base Software*. Presented at the Australian Computer Society conference. Available at: http://www.FBMf.eu

Pinker, Steven. [2007]. *The Stuff of Thought: Language as a Window into Human Nature*. New York, NY: Viking.

Ross, Ronald G. [1994, 1997]. *The Business Rule Book*. Business Rule Solutions, LLC.

Ross, Ronald G. [2003]. *Principles of the Business Rule Approach*. Boston, MA: Addison-Wesley.

Ross, Ronald G. [July 2007]. "What's Wrong with If-Then Syntax For Expressing Business Rules ~ One Size Doesn't Fit All," *Business Rules Journal*, Vol. 8, No. 7. Available at: http://www.BRCommunity.com/a2007/b353.html

Ross, Ronald G. [March 2008]. "The Emergence of SBVR and the True Meaning of 'Semantics': Why You Should Care (a Lot!) ~ Part 1," *Business Rules Journal*, Vol. 9, No. 3. Available at: http://www.BRCommunity.com/a2008/b401.html

Ross, Ronald G. with Lam, Gladys S.W. [2011]. *Building Business Solutions: Business Analysis with Business Rules*. Business Rule Solutions, LLC.

Semantics of Business Vocabulary and Business Rules (SBVR), (Version 1.0). [January 2008]. Object Management Group. Available at: http://www.omg.org/spec/SBVR/1.0/

Taylor, James and Neil Raden. [2007]. *Smart (Enough) Systems*. Boston, MA: Prentice-Hall.

Index

About the Author
Ronald G. Ross

Ronald G. Ross is recognized internationally as the "father of business rules." He serves as Executive Editor of Business Rules Community (www.BRCommunity.com) and its flagship publication, *Business Rules Journal*. He is a sought-after speaker at conferences world-wide. More than 50,000 people have heard him speak; many more than that have read his books. His popular seminars are given on-line through AttainingEdge and in Europe though IRM-UK.

Mr. Ross has served as Chair of the annual International Business Rules & Decisions Forum Conference since 1997. He was a charter member of the Business Rules Group (BRG) in the 1980s, and an editor of the two landmark BRG papers, *"The Business Motivation Model: Business Governance in a Volatile World"* and the *"Business Rules Manifesto."* He is active in OMG standards development, with core involvement in SBVR.

Mr. Ross is Principal and Co-Founder of Business Rule Solutions, LLC. At BRS, Mr. Ross co-develops *IPSpeak*™, its groundbreaking methodology for business rules, decision logic, and business vocabulary (concept models), including the popular *RuleSpeak*® (www.RuleSpeak.com). Mr. Ross is the author of nine professional books, including the ground-breaking, first book on business rules *The Business Rule Book* (1994) and *Principles of the Business Rule Approach*, Addison-Wesley (2003). His newest is *Building Business Solutions: Business Analysis with Business Rules* with Gladys S.W. Lam (2011, An IIBA® Sponsored Handbook). He holds a BA from Rice University and an MS in information science from Illinois Institute of Technology. For more information about Mr. Ross, visit www.RonRoss.info, which hosts his blog. Follow his tweets on Ronald_G_Ross.

About...

Business Rule Solutions, LLC — Business Rule Solutions, LLC is the recognized world leader in the advancement of business rules and decision management. Co-founders Ronald G. Ross and Gladys S.W. Lam are internationally acclaimed as the foremost experts and practitioners of related techniques and methodology.

   Since its inception in 1996, BRS has helped pilot the worldwide growth of business rules. BRS offers IPSpeak™, its groundbreaking methodology for business rules, decision logic, and business vocabulary (concept models), including the popular *RuleSpeak*®. Services include consulting, training, publications, and presentations. For more information about BRS, visit www.BRSolutions.com.

BRCommunity — Business Rules Community is a vertical, non-commercial community for business rule and decision management professionals, providing articles, expert commentary, panels, and a variety of other hands-on resources. BRCommunity.com and its flagship publication, *Business Rules Journal*, were established in 2000. Visit www.BRCommunity.com.

 #BRConcepts